S EARCHING FOR
S UMMER

A Solved but Unresolved
Missing Persons Case

By Anne Garrett Spry and
Brandy Shipp Rogge

SEARCHING FOR SUMMER

A Solved but Unresolved Missing Persons Case

Copyright 2019 by Anne Garrett Spry and Brandy Shipp Rogge

ISBN: 978-1-7330266-0-4

Published June 2019 by Personal Chapters LLC,
9512 Belleview Avenue
Kansas City, MO 64114
personalchapters@gmail.com

Table of Contents

Foreword

Violent crimes against women are nothing new in Kansas City.

In fact, the murder of ten "women of the evening" in this city led to my involvement in and the formation of the AdHoc Group Against Crime. That was in 1977.

AdHoc was all volunteer until 1988 when funding became available to hire a director and a small staff. In addition, a large group of volunteers came forward from the community, which really helped place AdHoc in a position to support the police in finding those responsible for the murder of these ten women and in solving other violent crimes.

After I served two four-year terms as city councilman and mayor pro-tem, I ran for the mayor's job in 2007 but lost by a little more than 3,000 votes. After the loss I was told I should restart the AdHoc Group Against Crime. AdHoc had been merged with another community-based organization called Project Neighborhood in 2000. The newly formed organization was called MoveUp. MoveUp dissolved in 2007, after which I was asked by many individuals and organizations, including representatives of the police department, county prosecutors and residents, to reorganize AdHoc. I did that in 2008.

I was active in all these efforts in 2004, and when Summer Shipp disappeared, her daughter and former husband contacted me. Ironically, I had known Summer prior to her disappearance while she was doing door-to-door market research in Independence, a city just east of Kansas City. I was shocked to learn of the mystery of her whereabouts and I set up a vigil where Summer was last seen. We put out flyers and worked with the Independence Police. I did radio and television appeals, some from the area where Summer was last seen. In fact, the name of the person eventually arrested and charged with her murder came to AdHoc's 24-hour community hotline. The name was turned over to Independence detectives.

As time passed, I participated in annual vigils and remembrances for Summer. I developed a relationship with her family and many of

Searching for Summer

Summer's friends, who, like me, were sickened to eventually learn what happened to her. How could someone be so inhuman as to do what was done to her and all the other victims we've had in this community who were dismembered?

When the trial of Summer's accused killer came up, I had planned to attend and offer support to the family but had a case in court representing the Kansas City Board of Police Commissioners, of which I am a member.

Summer's remains were found in 2007. In 2008 the "new" AdHoc had directed its focus to healing and justice; healing for the family and justice for the victim. We sometimes have three or four vigils in one day and someone suggested doing them on the anniversary dates of the disappearances, deaths or birthdates of the loved ones.

We were truly metropolitan in what we did for crime victims and their families, offering rewards that crossed state lines and all communities, regardless of their race or ethnicity. A crime victim is still a victim and the families desperately need help and healing from the horror of violence.

These kinds of cases are difficult. And I was so saddened to learn that the defendant in Summer's murder trial was acquitted due to lack of proof tying him to the evidence in the case. Sadly, few such crimes are ever solved or ever lead to convictions. But at least there is some satisfaction that just because he was acquitted doesn't mean he isn't guilty. And the accused killer is already serving a life sentence for another violent murder so he should never be able to commit another crime outside prison.

Summer Shipp, with her vibrant personality and large number of friends who loved her, was one of the more memorable cases we worked on. And like other victims, she deserves to be recognized and remembered for her life, not her violent death. I consider it an honor and a privilege to be able to help with that effort.

Alvin Brooks

Prologue

The image on the billboard towering over Interstate 35 captivated an entire city.

It certainly captured my attention.

You couldn't see her freckles in the photo of the woman that occupied a dominant corner of the billboard, but you could imagine them barely visible under that strawberry blonde hair. Just like you could empathize with the heartbreak that her family experienced as they orchestrated the placement of these signs, hundreds of flyers and appeals on utility poles and on the sides of taxicabs and metro buses: "Have you seen Summer Shipp?"

It could happen to any of us, any of our family members...the mysterious disappearance of a loved one. In 2016 more than 647,000 people went missing in the United States alone. Close to 37% of the cases are missing juveniles. At any given moment some 90,000 people are missing, with more than 50,000 of them adults. On average, three women are murdered every day in the U. S., and one of them is usually killed by an intimate partner. But violence against women by strangers is fairly rare. Summer Shipp must have been in the wrong place at the worst possible time, as we would all eventually discover.

I had covered a few missing persons cases in my career as a newspaper reporter, editor and publisher. And while the most agonizing of those cases involved missing children, Summer Shipp's case continued to haunt me long after her remains were found and her alleged killer identified.

A few months after my husband died, I had decided to do some energy efficiency projects in my home and stumbled across Ed Rogge's name on a contractor list maintained by my neighborhood association. He was working in my basement one day, sealing some foundation cracks, when his wife came down the stairs. Ed introduced me to Brandy Shipp Rogge and the hair on my arms stood up.

"Are you Summer Shipp's daughter?" I asked. She replied in the affirmative. Later I asked Ed if Brandy had ever been approached about writing a book about her mother. He said several writers had asked Brandy about that, but she had never been ready.

Searching for Summer

I believe the goosebumps I experienced the day I met Brandy Shipp Rogge were a divine confirmation that a major project would be forthcoming. At the time I was just getting started on my new retirement vocation of helping people preserve their life stories through memoir. But most of my clients, including wonderful people like Kansas City icon Mamie Hughes Rodgers, were still alive. How would I help someone preserve the memories of a deceased family member?

With Summer Shipp, we found the answer in her friends. This wonderful woman had a gift for bringing together diverse and fascinating people and making them feel like they were the most important folks on earth. And what a rich legacy this Summer Shipp left in her friends' heart-warming stories of her antics and personality traits! In fact, her closest friends still gather on a regular basis to have lunch or a crazy hat party and recall her memory. They call themselves "Summer's Girls."

This book about Summer is as much a collection of stories about an unusual woman as it is a frustrating true crime saga. Frustrating because her alleged killer was acquitted. But that's getting ahead of our story.

Right now I want to introduce you to Summer Shipp and take you on a journey into a story that has lessons for us all. In the following pages you will be witness to a love that drives friends and family to never give up hope; to persist against all odds when a loved one goes missing. You will also be witness to a high-profile disappearance that is ultimately solved, but sadly, not resolved.

Anne Garrett Spry

1-Brandy's Nightmares Return

December 2016

The nightmares and flashbacks have started again.

Even though it's been 12 years since the disappearance of her mother, Brandy Shipp Rogge still carries the pain. It is visceral, never-ending, and nothing ever seems to excise it.

Sure, she can distract herself. Every time she and husband Ed witness the birth of another litter of their Pug puppies, Brandy fiercely focuses her love and attention on those squirming, adorable creatures. She almost chains herself to the house until they're old enough to sell and go to new homes. That is, except for the times the Rogges take a new litter to a local nursing home, or to the bank, post office or even Home Depot, and let the employees fuss over the darling babies. She loves seeing delight and adoration light up the faces of everyone who cuddles one of their pups.

Brandy never had a baby of her own...just lots of Pug babies. She had been her mother's only child and Summer had doted on Brandy the same way she now coos and kisses these fur babies. Even as an adult, Brandy's mother had made excuses for her while boasting with pride about how beautiful she had become in her young adulthood.

But now the latest news has brought back the nightmares, adding to the agony that her insomnia and multiple health challenges always bring during the bleak hours before dawn.

Brandy knows how the families of Kara Kopetsky and Jessica Runions feel and what they are going through now. She has read the headlines and seen the television reports that two skulls have been found in the woods only two miles from Belton High School. One of them has been identified positively as Jessica Runions, who disappeared in 2016.

In 2007 Kara Kopetsky disappeared from that same high school. Now her mother will have to be patient for maybe another year while DNA tests are conducted on the second skull found in the same woods where Jessica's remains were found.

Upon hearing the news reports about the two skulls, Brandy immediately recalls the overseas phone messages she had received right after she had moved to Poland with Jeff. The messages reported a fisherman had found her mother's skeletal remains in the Little Blue River, some three years after her disappearance. Brandy also recalls the endless trips all over the country, the television appearances, news conferences, vigils and her evolution into the role of a national advocate for families with missing loved ones.

Brandy's mind races around all the images and events that the recent headlines have brought to mind in her own family's tragedy: The frenetic search activity by friends and family, the sorting through of clues and setting up of a reward fund, the memorial tributes, the civil lawsuit against the marketing company her mother worked for that had sent her out alone to conduct surveys in a rough neighborhood in Independence, Missouri. And finally, the official funeral and burial.

Brandy feels compelled to reach out to the latest traumatized family. She and her dad had already visited Kara Kopetsky's mother soon after her daughter's disappearance. After all, they belonged to the same club now. They were bonded by the dubious connections shared by families of missing persons.

Brandy picks up the phone, dreading the call she is about to make, but realizing how important it is. She also knows Summer is probably watching from above, nodding her head and smiling in sweet approval.

Chapter 2 - Summer and Brandy

December 3, 2004

Brandy Shipp fidgets on the edge of the antique barber chair in her mother's living room. The 33-year-old striking redhead had let herself in a few minutes before to ask Summer's advice about cleaning the floors in her new house. As a confirmed workaholic who puts in 60 to 80 hours a week, Brandy has always enjoyed the services of a housekeeper. But no longer. Suddenly she is faced with doing unfamiliar household chores.

As usual, her mother is not alone today. Two older women sit on the long, threadbare couch in the living room of the house in the city's Valentine neighborhood. The thick, gray stones of the three-story dwelling are typical of this gentrified section of town near the University of Missouri's Kansas City campus.

"Brandy and I moved here a few years after her dad and I divorced," Summer Shipp is explaining to the women, after they have commented on the house and her decorating style.

"I had just gotten out from under the Bijou Theater and was trying to figure out how to support myself," she continues explaining to her guests. "Do you remember the Bijou?"

Brandy finally joins the conversation because the one-screen movie theater her dad had left Summer in the legal separation was so close to her heart.

"We were the first theater in the Midwest to show the Rocky Horror Picture Show continuously," she says proudly, and tries to explain the appeal of the cult movie to the older women, both of whom have blank looks on their faces.

Without giving the women a chance to learn about that bit of cultural history, Summer quickly explains that she had purchased this house knowing she could take in university students to help pay the mortgage. What she didn't explain, muses Brandy, is that in return for the students' help paying her bills, the 55-year-old Summer listens to their problems and gives them motherly advice and sympathy–just like she is doing now with one of the two women.

Summer focuses on the woman she introduces to Brandy as Leanne. Leanne's sister, Evelyn, one of Summer's neighbors, has brought her here thinking a visit to this vivacious little woman will cheer her up. So far it's working. From the conversation that she only half listens to, Brandy learns Leanne is battling an aggressive form of cancer. She is obviously weak and sick from chemo treatments. Brandy stirs uneasily and watches her mother closely for the telltale signs that Summer will soon be "adopting" another elderly person to care for and cater to.

Summer is good at that. In fact, Brandy's mother had recently taken care of funeral arrangements for an older friend of her ex-boyfriend, Jim. Jim had introduced Summer to Don Berger at John Knox Village in Lee's Summit. Don and Jim's mother had been faithful companions at the Village, but she died, leaving Don lonely and heartbroken.

Not to worry. Summer took an instant liking to the older gentleman, just as she had many other seniors with health issues, or just plain loneliness. She immediately began regular visits to Don, sometimes twice a week, much to the amazement of the nurses and staff at The Village. So many of their residents had no visitors, but Don had Summer, a complete stranger, coming regularly. And Don's distant family was shocked when Summer recruited her strange musician friend, "Reverend" Dwight Frizzel, to conduct Don's recent funeral service. They had been too busy and lived too far away to handle the arrangements. But they all agreed it was a beautiful, perfect service. Summer and Frizzel had picked out one of Don's favorite tunes from his extensive record collection for the service music. *Blue Skies,* Brandy remembers. The music seemed to cause everyone at the service to release their tears. Even she had cried and she barely knew the man.

Now Brandy wonders if this cancer patient in Summer's living room will be a replacement for Don. Summer focuses all her attention on Leanne and wants to know everything Leanne is going through. Summer doesn't let her gaze wander in boredom or pain, like so many other people do when Leanne recounts her medical challenges. In fact, Leanne gets the feeling that Summer is almost radiating healing into her soul with those intense, blue eyes.

Summer sits erect, while managing to appear totally relaxed on the edge of an antique wheelchair she had found at a flea market and painted a brilliant shade of tropical turquoise. Brandy glances around at the rest of the crazy but comfortable surroundings, still watching her mother surreptitiously. Nothing matches in this room, or in the rest of the house. In addition to the improbable wheelchair, there is the antique barber chair Brandy now perches in. It has always been a conversation starter with visitors. In another corner, a bright pink beauty parlor chair, complete with attached hairdryer, provides another spot of color and attention. Summer had converted an antique glass door into a coffee table in the center of the living room. A long bench, probably an old church pew that Summer had picked up at a garage sale, sits just below the stairway leading to the second floor. But no one can sit on the bench because it is loaded with at least 50 antique purses.

The entire first floor of this house looks like a funky antique boutique. And the owner of the house holds court here with a sophistication that seems incongruent with the innocent sincerity she always exhibits. Her strawberry blonde curls form a short halo of sunshine around her face. And while she doesn't like for anyone to make her out to be bigger than life, Summer reigns over her surroundings like a benevolent sprite, in a room that her daughter has always found welcoming and peaceful.

Brandy nervously twirls a tendril of her flaming auburn hair, impatiently poised for flight and ready to leave for one of her three jobs.

Finally, Brandy stands up and the two visitors notice she towers a head above her mother. Brandy favors her father, John, in stature and temperament. She is as driven and energetic as her mother is serene and laid back. Right now Brandy needs to get her mother's advice on cleaning the house she has just purchased. The floors are laminate and she has no clue how to clean them.

Sensing her daughter's impatience, Summer places a reassuring arm around Brandy's waist and addresses the two visitors. "I want you to know that I only had one child because I could not imagine loving anyone else as much as I love her. She is absolutely beautiful, don't you think?"

Brandy rolls her eyes in embarrassment and puts her head in her hands at hearing the same words Summer tells everyone. True, she has enjoyed the self-esteem that comes from a mother's unceasing adoration. But then she recalls her dad saying Summer used almost the same words about her little dog, a feisty wire-haired terrier named "Annie Annie," just before Brandy was born. "She was so worried she didn't have enough love for the dog and a baby," John had recalled with a chuckle.

And even now, Summer's dogs get all the love and attention when Brandy isn't around. Brandy loves animals too, but would never make a sick dog live long after it should have been put down, the way her mother has in the past. Neither would she immediately adopt an animal that happens to wander into the yard as Summer has, too many times to count.

Summer just seems to collect lost animals and people. It's like some magnetic force pulls them into the all-encompassing rays of sunshine she puts out. Brandy recalls the time Summer had gone with Sue Herrick to work on a research study and they met Sue's mother at Long John Silver's for lunch. Later, Sue told Brandy how Summer had patiently, and without embarrassment, fed her mother, who suffered from Alzheimer's.

Right now Summer is focusing her attention on Leanne and her cancer challenges.

But Brandy needs to get to work. These women can keep talking to Summer after she leaves.

"Mom, excuse me for interrupting, but I need to know how I should clean the floors in my new house. Then I'll leave you alone and get back to work."

Summer looks at her daughter gratefully. It's not often Brandy seeks her advice. In fact, she often assumes the symbolic role of a child in Brandy's company, partly because of her daughter's stature and also because Summer's essence is childlike innocence and curiosity.

"I'll show you how to clean those floors!" Summer says with enthusiasm. She motions for the three women to follow her to the kitchen, stopping first at the stereo to hit the start button on a Marvin Gaye CD.

As the women watch, Summer pulls two dish towels out of a drawer. All three stand open-mouthed as she ties them on her bare feet. She next pulls a bottle of Dawn off the kitchen counter and dribbles the blue liquid all over the floor of the galley kitchen. She turns on the water in the sink, grabs the spray nozzle and squirts water on top of the dish soap.

As they all listen to the refrain of "Ain't No Mountain High Enough," Summer and the two older women start head bobbing to the Motown sound they all grew up with. Summer moves her rag-tied feet through the soapy water. By the time Marvin Gaye' starts in on "You've Got What It Takes" on the 1967 United album, all four women dissolve into helpless laughter, especially Leanne. It has been years since she laughed this hard.

Summer's mouth turns up in a self-deprecating grin, but she keeps grooving in the suds. When "You've Got What It Takes" ends and the changed pace of "I Could Build My Whole World Around You" starts playing, she pulls the rags off her feet, wrings them out in the sink and rinses them. Then she sprays more water on the floor and does the rinse cycle rag dance to laughter that's only slightly more subdued than during the wash cycle.

"It's clean, isn't it?" Summer asks her appreciative audience. "And it's exercise! Clean your floors and work out at the same time. What could be better?" She directs her question to her daughter, who sighs and shakes her head, knowing she will never clean her floors that way.

"Mom, I gotta go!" she says with a grin.

"I'll follow you out," says Summer, putting on a pair of ballet slippers she wears around the house, letting the laces trail behind her. She tosses the towels into the sink and steps around the puddles to escort her visitors to the front door, grabbing a jacket off the pile of purses on the church pew. Leanne's laughter and the walk over to Summer's has worn her out and she needs to get home and rest before her chemo treatment in the morning. Summer has already offered to take her to the treatment center if her sister can't.

As Brandy trails slightly behind, Summer gives Leanne a hug of encouragement, as if she were an old friend. In fact, Leanne feels that this is true. Summer has made her feel like the most important person in the room today, and the visit has made her temporarily forget her cancer. What a ray of sunshine is this Summer Shipp!

Leanne and Evelyn wave goodbye. Brandy has a hand on the handle of her car door but feels her mother's hand cover hers.

"Don't go," Summer pleads. "Not yet. You have to stop and smell my roses."

Brandy rolls her eyes again in impatience. "Mom, I smell them every time I'm over here! Besides, they're dead. It's winter."

"But they're still beautiful, even though they're old and faded. Right? Smell them anyway and imagine what they'll be like in the spring," she teases, searching for anything to delay saying goodbye.

"Whatever you say, Mom" Brandy relents. "They are always beautiful, even in the winter. But I gotta go. I've got to get the house cleaned tonight because I'm hosting that bachelorette party tomorrow night."

"That's right," smiles her mother. "I forgot. But I don't know how you'll even be able to enjoy your new place when you're working three jobs. I worry about you spreading yourself too thin. You might get sick."

"And I worry about you going off by yourself in your marketing job. I don't think you should be doing that alone, and all your friends agree with me," counters Brandy. "Besides, you know I'm a crazy workaholic and I want to continue taking you on vacations that I can afford myself," she says, waving a good-bye.

Summer doesn't really need her daughter's financial help so much anymore. She does go out to eat occasionally with her new boyfriend,

who must find it easy and inexpensive to entertain her, especially since she's vegetarian. It doesn't take much food to fill her five foot slim frame anyway. The tabbouleh and bouillabaisse that she fixes at home all the time are enough to satisfy her small appetite in between dates.

Her frugal eating habits have come from growing up poor in Granite City, Illinois. Her mother, Cora, had done the best she could to raise Summer and her three brothers after their alcoholic father left them, coming back into their lives only occasionally. Summer shudders and pushes those memories out of her mind. The poverty and shame she has lived through were part of the motivation for changing her given name of Dolores to Summer after she and John had married. She had taken on a totally new identity when she left Granite City, picking Kansas City by opening a road map and favoring the place because it had the fewest "curvy" streets, as she was quite directionally challenged. Besides, it seemed a satisfying distance away from her difficult childhood and from the trouble her brothers always seemed to be getting into with the police.

Her religion is about the only thing Summer brought with her to Kansas City from her old life. Cora raised her as a Jehovah's Witness and, despite never attending services now, Summer continues to practice the tenets of her faith, at least where holiday celebrations are concerned. The Shipps never celebrated Christmas or Halloween the way Brandy's little friends did, but Summer always showered her with gifts all the other days of the year. Every day is a holiday in Summer's eyes. And she has a habit of buying her friends gifts on her own birthday.

Aside from her gift-buying habits, Summer's rough childhood has made her extremely frugal–to the point where she had to be forced to spend money on herself as a young married woman. She recalls the time in the 1970s when she drooled over a $300 pair of red cowboy boots in Las Vegas, and John insisted she buy them. She had cringed at the price tag. But she still has those boots and wears them occasionally.

Summer climbs the front steps, trailed by her dogs, Alex and Miles, and goes back inside, a little lonely now that the house is empty, except for the student boarders upstairs. She scratches Miles, a blind and partially deaf, scruffy-looking mop that she has rescued. Alex decides he wants her attention and places a white paw on her shoulder, whimpering for attention. She kisses his cheek and tousles the hair on his head, putting her feet on the coffee table and settling into the sofa with a sigh as she again realizes how lucky she is to be living this life, in this house, and enjoying the friendship of some amazing people. She is truly a rich woman spiritually, she tells herself for probably the millionth time. But it wasn't always so.

Summer retrieves a more pleasant memory of her young adulthood; the chapter of her life when she miraculously fell into luxury by marrying John Shipp and then giving birth to her precious Brandy.

John had just been transferred to Kansas City from Florida in 1969 as the manager for the local Metro Goldwyn Mayer branch. He was living in an apartment at 4010 Oak Street. Summer was known then as Dolores Irene Burns and she had been in Kansas City for a few months when she visited a friend at that apartment complex. Her yellow bikini immediately caught John's eye. Even though he was seriously dating a nurse, he started dating Dolores too.

By October of 1970 Dolores was pregnant. She gave John the news the night he took her to see the screening of *2001: A Space Odyssey*, before it was released to the public, one of the fringe benefits of his job. Years later he recalled of that night's announcement, "We decided to move in together and see if we were simpatico."

The Oak Street apartment became their first home, and since their front door was just a few feet away from the pool, John "worked" in the water with a phone nearby. When it rang, he'd pull himself to the side, pick up the receiver and negotiate film exhibition contracts for the hundreds of theaters in Missouri and Kansas. Dee, as he called her then, had been working for Bendix prior to meeting John, and living in a little upstairs apartment in the 4500 block of Harrison.

They got married in a civil ceremony at the courthouse with John's brother and a friend of Dee's as witnesses. They soon moved from Oak into a cozy cottage at 4911 Baltimore in the Plaza area. Two years later they moved to a nice duplex that also had a pool. Kansas City Chiefs football player Ed Podolak lived in the other half of their unit.

Brandy was a few years old when Dolores decided to reinvent herself. Brandy's middle name is Alexis, so Dee started calling herself Summer Alexis Shipp, adopting the name through common usage, as the family attorney advised at the time.

John had been "empire building" in those years. He had left MGM and bought a small independent film distribution company called Thomas Films. He changed the name to Thomas & Shipp Films, Inc. and started making more money than he had ever dreamed of. Since John had come from a humble background himself, and like Summer was the child of an alcoholic parent, he began spending like he had just won the lottery.

By the time Brandy was three years old, John was making $200,000 a year. In 1974 he bought a beautiful old home at 620 E. 54th Street in the Crestwood neighborhood. The lovely two-story English Tudor had a sauna, art gallery, gym and the biggest private pool in Kansas City at that time.

In those heady days John spent a lot of time on both coasts and began a lifestyle that included drugs and $100 bottles of Dom Perignon for breakfast. Along the way, he developed about a $20,000 a year cocaine and pills habit. He now realizes that he had an arrogance then that assumed rules did not apply to him.

At first, Summer had kept quiet about her husband's grandiose lifestyle and funneled most of her love and attention to her daughter. But she was admittedly dazed by it all–especially when John whisked her and Brandy to the Cannes Film Festival in 1976. They checked into the Gran Hotel du Cap Antibes, spending time with David Caradine, Cary Grant and other celebrities. As the festival ended, the Shipps took an extended vacation, going to London and staying at the Dorchester, then to the Excelsior in Rome and back to Paris, this time staying at the Ritz. Summer recalls that a driver picked them up at every stop on the trip. They returned to the U.S. on the first-ever Air France Concorde flight from Paris to Washington, D.C. That was May 24, 1976.

Poor country folks living like kings. That's how John later described those years, and that certainly rings true for Summer. While the couple rubbed elbows with Paul Newman, JoannE Woodward, Tim Conway and Clint Eastwood, and John became one of the biggest independent film distributors in the country, Summer somehow kept her feet on the ground. Even though the Shipps had a beautiful home, and a new Cadillac every year, Summer didn't change. While John was jet-setting all over the country, she stayed home and doted on Brandy, singing to her, reading books and inviting other children over for play dates. She also managed to find time to volunteer at the Crittendon Center, a residence for emotionally disturbed young women. She often brought three or four of the girls to the house to swim, a coveted privilege that only the best behavior could grant to these young women, many of whom had never been near a pool.

Searching for Summer

Still, her marriage with John suffered from his absence and his drug and drinking habits. Laughing at the memory, she recalls the one time she expressed her frustration and anger at him, throwing a whole cantaloupe at him in the kitchen and barely missing his head.

One of the final breaks in their relationship occurred at a Christmas party in the late 1970s. John's bankers had been invited and went into his office during the party to find a pile of cocaine on his desk. John and other partiers had been indulging in that pile all night. The bankers looked at the hill of white powder, looked at John, turned around and walked out of the room quietly. They never called him on his habit. He was, after all, one of their best customers, bringing in between two and four million in cash a year.

By that time though, the film company was in a decline. The smaller films John distributed were now being pursued by major film companies and Shipp was so highly leveraged that he was among the first to hit bottom. By then Summer and John had split up once and he had moved to an apartment in the trendy Plaza area for a few months. They soon got back together, but the end was inevitable.

Summer remembers that a business friend, Jack Poessiger, had convinced John to visit Berlin and Liepzig, Germany. When he got back to Kansas City after ten days overseas, Summer told him immediately she wanted out of the marriage. Her jet-lagged, doped-up husband was convinced he would not live another year anyway, and Summer's announcement was more than he could bear. As he told someone years later, "I viewed myself as a young prince who had to leave for a few years and come back later to reclaim my kingdom." Now he knows that perspective was total "balderdash."

John left within the next 72 hours. This was October of 1980. He was close to being broke. He left his attorney in charge of closing businesses and using assets to settle his debts, as far as possible. He had wanted Summer and Brandy to come with him, but Summer declined. With his mind reeling in confusion, he just drove. When he stopped, Shipp found himself in the community of Pass-A-Grille, Florida, the southernmost tip of St. Pete Beach. The Gulf of Mexico lay to the south and west and Boca Ciega Bay to the east. Sitting on the pier at the city-owned Pass-A-Grille Bait Shop and Charter Boat Service, John decided this was as good a place as any to start a new life. He made arrangements with the city to lease the bait shop and pier, then immersed himself in the fisherman's culture. He got around with a bicycle. Slowly he healed and de-toxed.

Brandy soon came to spend summers and school holidays with him, while John and Summer maintained a cordial relationship. But in the summer of 1983, the "No-Name Storm," a ferocious tropical disturbance, raged down on St. Pete Beach and dumped the Pass-A-Grille Bait Shop and Charter Boat Service into Boca Ciega Bay. While the pier was destroyed, the storm did not destroy John Shipp. In fact, living on the water's edge had given him strength and he was soon on his way back to a good life and great career. The separation with his wife continued, however, despite their cordial relationship.

What Summer got out of the marriage was a $2,000 a month stipend for two years from a business John had sold. She also got the deed to the Bijou Theater in Westport. John had purchased it early in his career but never made money on the one-screen movie house. However, the theater had developed a cult following by playing The Rocky Horror Picture Show every Friday and Saturday night for 52 weeks a year, along with other classic movies on the schedule.

Summer smiles at the memory. She had loved the Bijou and schmoozing with the customers. In fact, she had met some of her best friends at the ticket window during the few years she owned and managed the theater.

Summer shakes her head now, recalling how naïve and inexperienced she was to think she could be successful at a business that was already declining. But she had tackled the task with enthusiasm, until the day the lease expired on the building the theater operated in. That's when Jerry Harrington acquired the business and renamed it The Tivoli. Later, when the three-screen movie house across the street became available, Jerry moved the Tivoli there.

Even then, when John came to Kansas City for visits, he thought the three of them could still be a family. But Summer had begun to appreciate her independence. The actual divorce didn't occur until John met Naomi, his current wife. John and Summer signed divorce documents in 1988.

To try to support herself during the separation and after losing the Bijou, Summer cleaned houses and did odd jobs. She also started taking items to flea markets to sell. And now she had the market research work. She loved having a "license" to ask people about themselves, expanding on the rote questions the corporate clients wanted answered. If there was a way to dig out more information besides a consumer's beverage preferences or favorite pizza combination, Summer Shipp would find it. And her clients would often be charmed enough by Summer to seek information about her and pursue a friendship. But no matter where she went and whether or not a friendship developed from a survey, her subjects always remembered her.

Tomorrow Summer would have an hour-long marketing survey she needed to conduct in nearby Independence, contacting as many households as she could manage.

She decides it's time to head upstairs to get ready for bed. Alex trails behind her while Miles gets a ride upstairs in Summer's arms. As the day dims, Summer thinks again about how far she has come from Granite City, Illinois and a life of poverty. She slides into bed with a smile on her face. She has so much to look forward to and is just downright happy with her life, even if she sometimes worries a little about how to pay her bills. Tomorrow will probably bring her some good commissions. She is confident she might even complete four or five interviews. The hard part is just getting her prospects to allow her to sit down with them. If she gets in the door, she's home free.

Chapter 3 - Assignment: Independence

December 8, 2004 - Morning

Summer settles her coffee mug on the worn seat of her aging BMW, trying not to spill coffee on her purse. Maybe, she thinks, she should buy one of those cupholder things, since the console of the car is full of other items, leaving no room for the mug.

She grins at herself in the rearview mirror, thinking about how many times a stop at the local Starbucks has made her late for things.

Today, it doesn't really matter what time she arrives in the Independence neighborhood she has been assigned by Roper Worldwide. After all, her door-to-door market research isn't driven by deadlines. Roper pays her by the completed surveys she turns in and the New York-based company allows about an hour per interview. She has all day.

Summer has been doing this kind of work for years. Sometimes the research that she and her colleagues conduct in shopping malls is as trifling and superficial as taste tests for carbonated soft drinks. Other times, like today's survey, the interviews seek more in-depth information that might include consumer attitudes about products or their behaviors while using them. These surveys have to be done in the consumer's homes.

Summer always laughs away the concerns of her daughter and friends about the safety of going door to door, insisting there is no danger. She's good at this work because she is a good listener, or so her friends tell her. Funny, but her mother had always said the same thing, always adding that Summer had been that way since a young child. Summer misses her mom so much. Cora had died just a few short months ago. Now Summer wishes she could call her mom or send her some little treat in the mail, just to let her know she is thinking of her and loves her. Summer had already let her mother know, years before, that she didn't blame her for the rough upbringing Summer and her brothers had in Granite City. And maybe some of what she now does unconsciously with her interview subjects, and even with her scores of friends, is seeking affirmation and approval. The sincere and focused interest she showers on friends and total strangers is perhaps a way to affirm and test the new identity she chose for herself when she came to Kansas City so many years ago. She hasn't been Dolores Irene Burns for decades, but the insecurities of a dysfunctional childhood still have a way of leaking out in her constant need for approval.

Summer shakes herself from the reverie and takes a satisfying sip of coffee, focusing anew on her driving. She's on Independence Avenue now, also known as Highway 24, skirting the north side of the historic city. Independence had once been the jumping off place for steamboats going up and down down the Missouri River, and for the wagon trains that headed west on the Santa Fe, California and Oregon Trails.

She has just passed the part of the avenue that is infamous for its average of four prostitutes for every three or four blocks. She shudders involuntarily at the thought of so many hopeless, lost souls, subjected to so much violence and forced slavery. Summer always pushes away thoughts of the evil, perverse side of humanity. She prefers to look for the good in others. If she doesn't acknowledge evil, it doesn't exist.

In the distance she sees the elaborate silver spire of the Community of Christ Church Temple rising like an improbable, futuristic embellishment on the landscape.

In the 1830s Independence had become a place of mob violence and religious persecution. Some of its inhabitants drove out a group of settlers, who were members of the Church of Jesus Christ of Latter-day Saints, pushing them north across the Missouri River. The settlers' leader, Joseph Smith Jr., had planned to erect a temple and establish a "New Jerusalem" in Independence. Two decades after Smith's shooting in Carthage, Illinois and the exodus of his followers from Missouri, then later from Illinois and on to Utah, splinter groups like The Church of Christ Temple Lot and the Reorganized Church of Latter-day Saints (now known as the Community of Christ) had returned to Independence.

Summer could understand religious persecution. After all, she had grown up as a Jehovah's Witness. She recalls how people sometimes visibly cringed when she accompanied her mother to knock on doors in Granite City and hand them a Watchtower publication. She was used to having doors slammed in her face. But in those days, accompanying her mother on evangelism trips was like an outing. And her presence was sometimes the opening Cora needed to be invited into someone's house. That was Summer's favorite event. It gave her a chance to see how other people lived. If she was lucky, the homeowner might even offer them a glass of iced tea or a piece of candy.

Maybe it was those good memories, which were so rare in her troubled childhood, that made Summer enjoy her marketing work so much. It feels so familiar, and somehow comforting, to go to a door and give the person who opens it her famous smile. She tries not to take it personally when a prospective interview subject rudely tells her to go mind her own business.

On this brisk December day, despite the fact that Summer will not celebrate the holiday that's quickly approaching, she absolutely loves the atmosphere that precedes Christmas. It means special gatherings with friends and fun shopping excursions. Her friends might be buying gifts for their families, but she tags along and window shops, a favorite hobby of hers. And of course, there is a big party on her calendar to look forward to. Her friend Susan, whose family owns an art gallery in Westport, will be celebrating her 65th birthday anniversary with a huge bash. All Summer's precious friends will be there. She can't wait.

Summer parks on West College and glances at the little stick-on calendar on the dash of the BMW that her friend Norma Jean had sold to her. She circles the date, December 8, 2004, then exits the car. This sleepy street of modest, even rundown homes, will be her conference room for the day.

This is not the first time she's worked in Independence. She does not mind its former reputation as the methamphetamine capital of Missouri. She just views this neighborhood as she does Mission Hills or Prairie Village. Crime statistics seldom enter her mind.

Summer checks the clipboard that holds the addresses of her interview subjects and the forms she'll be filling out. She ties her warm red scarf more tightly around her neck against the December chill and brushes a few breakfast muffin crumbs off her jeans. She squares her shoulders, lifts her chin in determination and steps onto the first front porch. It will be a good day. She's certain of it.

Chapter 4 - The Empath at Nick's

December 4, 2004 - *afternoon*

Malisa Jennings pauses her bar rag in mid-swipe but continues a conversation with her good friend, Chris Thornhill. He is a regular at Nick's Tavern, but the two men walking in now are not. Yet there is something familiar about one of them.

As they take a seat at the far end of the bar, Malisa acknowledges them with a nod but soon pauses in talking to Chris, telling him she'll return to their conversation shortly.

"What can I get you boys?" she asks as she walks their way. But the two have their heads together and she hears the younger man say, "What do you think," as he looks at her.

"Yep, she's everything you told me she was," the older man replies, giving Malisa a look that travels from her blond hair down her five foot, slim frame, to the tips of her cowboy boots. That comment causes her to shudder involuntarily.

The shudder soon turns to near panic as she looks into the eyes of the younger man. "Those eyes were so empty," she would later tell a police detective.

Malisa's lifelong sensibilities as an empath, senses that had saved her life on many occasions, are on high alert, sounding all kinds of alarm bells. She recognizes this man as one who had come in by himself a few weeks before looking like a homeless man. On that occasion he had been dressed in gray sweatpants and a ratty sweatshirt. He had ordered a draft beer, saying it was the first time he'd had one in six years. He had downed two draws and left.

Today Malisa cautiously serves two bottles of beer to the men who introduce themselves as Jeffrey Sauerbry and his neighbor, Paul Loral. She mentally curses her boss for deciding just a few days before not to serve beer on tap anymore. She hopes this doesn't cause a scene with these two guys, especially since her psychological antennae are screaming at her to keep from angering them for any reason.

In fact, her anger at her boss now focuses on the fact that he had once again left her by herself to serve the afternoon customers. Thank God Chris was still here. She begins pacing behind the bar and eyeing the telephone, ready to punch in 911 if anything happens. Something is just not right with those two.

Malisa's discomfort is soon confirmed as Sauerbry and Loral get up to go to the bathroom together, something she's never seen two men do before in this bar, or ever, for that matter.

While they're gone, she rushes to Chris to let him know her fears and begs him to stay.

The two men soon return and focus on Chris, trying to intimidate him into leaving by standing on each side of him and making pointed remarks about it being time for him to go back to his job. All the while they both badger Malisa to play pool with them. As they begin pacing around the pool table, the way she had been pacing behind the bar, the two hold whispered consultations and both look at their watches.

Finally, the men sit down again at the bar to down their second round of beer, still whispering, still occasionally looking at their watches. Suddenly they both stand up to leave and Sauerbry walks over to the waitress station where Malisa has been hovering close to the phone. He offers his hand to shake and she reluctantly accepts the gesture. Immediately she regrets it, as he grabs her forearm with his other hand and pulls hard. She feels her knees buckling and knows that he is capable of pulling her right over the top of the bar. She starts to reach wildly for the phone with her free hand. Just then he releases her, saying, "It's all right. It's probably better that you didn't anyway."

She quakes inside to think what he might mean. As the two men walk out of Nick's, tears course down Malisa's cheeks and her inner trembling increases to whole-body, outward intensity.

She does not know that today won't be the last time she sees Jeffrey Sauerbry. Neither does she know that her life is about to change forever because of those empty black eyes and those cruelly strong arms.

Chapter 5 - The Art Gallery Birthday Party

December 10, 2004

Tonight will be a milestone for Susan Lawrence. She has invited almost everyone she knows to Pi Art Gallery on 18th Street to celebrate her 65th birthday anniversary.

It wasn't so much that she thinks everyone would want to celebrate her 65th, as much as it is the fact that she had found the perfect invitation. It appealed to the art aesthetic that she had absorbed through her DNA. She just has to share the occasion and the venue with all her friends and acquaintances. And she knows a lot of people in Kansas City, a network she has at least partially inherited from her parents.

The Lawrences had moved to Kansas City in 1949. Susan's dad, Sidney, left his job as an art historian and teacher at NYU to come to the Midwest to serve as director of community relations for the Jewish Federation. When he retired Sidney taught art history at Rockhurst College. Susan's mother, Anne, ran the family art gallery at 43rd and Main.

The Lawrence Gallery went through many incarnations, including becoming the Lawrence Gallery and Coffee House in the 1960s, after Susan's dad came home from San Francisco with an espresso machine. When the family sold the location on Main, it became The Vanguard, but retained its coffee house identity. The sidewalk in that location still bears the name "Lawrence Gallery," so her family heritage is literally etched into the Kansas City landscape.

Susan helped cement the family legacy when she went into business with her mother, founded the Westport Gallery Association and began First Fridays, an activity that highlights the importance of art and promotes local galleries. By 1984 her mother retired and Susan secured a business partner, Sally Batz. The studio that showed European and American art then became known as the Batz/Lawrence Gallery.

And so it is fitting for the woman who still owns the trade name "Susan Lawrence Fine Art" to hold her birthday party in an art gallery.

Her excitement expands as she rushes into the Pi with her family members and an armload of music CDs. Her talented friend, Beau Bledsoe, was to have provided the music tonight, but had apologetically cancelled due to a family emergency. Thus the CDs. But Susan is used to improvising and rolling with the unexpected. She has found someone to take charge of the music so she is free to mingle with her guests.

Despite her anticipation of the enjoyable evening ahead, something nags at Susan . . . a vague uneasiness that creeps into her stomach each time a friend calls to ask if she has heard from Summer, or if Summer has said she is coming to the party.

"You know Summer never gives an RSVP," she had told all the callers. "If it's a party, and if it's one of her friends, she'll be there."

And all night she expects to look up and see Summer's strawberry blonde hair appear above her constant cup of Starbucks (she always claims to be allergic to alcohol). She will breeze in with her tinkling laugh and immediately draw a circle of male and female fans, all eager to bask in her energy.

Susan had been so busy getting ready for this party, picking up her sister from Philadelphia, looking over the shoulders of her chef daughter-in-law while she made the most incredible birthday cake, that she has pushed aside worries about Summer.

But as the evening wears on with no sign of her friend, Susan's unease turns to overt worry. Then Scotti and Linda come to the party with the news that they have been trying all day to reach Summer, without success. Those two are among Summer's closest confidantes, even taking her with them on a recent trip to Jamaica.

Jerry Wheeler is worried too. He keeps leaving the party to make phone calls, then returns and shakes his head "No." He cannot reach Summer on the phone.

It is not like their friend to miss a party.

Even as Susan circulates with her guests, plying them with appetizers and drinks, even after she opens gifts and everyone eats cake, her ears tune into every conversation that mentions Summer.

This gallery is full of "Summer people" tonight–the eclectic, artsy types that she seems to collect almost like she collects her funky antiques.

You couldn't help but love the woman. Susan first met Summer at a Westport business networking event. That was when she still owned the

Bijou Theater. Shortly afterwards Summer invited Susan to a garden party at her house in the Valentine neighborhood.

Those garden parties are just the best! The women who attend them bond through their liberal politics, their love of art and their fondness for Kansas City. They enjoy each other so much that they started going out to dinner once a month to continue cultivating the friendships and good times. Like any good, organic group of women, they talk about their children, their lives, what they are reading or listening to, what they are doing on weekends. So when something isn't right with one of them, they all go into worry mode.

Susan Lawrence has a wonderful 65th birthday anniversary. The party leaves her with many fond memories. But the night will also be forever etched in her recollections as the night that everyone realizes Summer Shipp is missing.

Chapter 6 – The Search Begins

December 10, 2004

Brandy Shipp is out running errands and picking up supplies for the Christmas luncheon for her employer, The International Brotherhood of Iron Workers Local #10 in North Kansas City. She scrambles for the cellphone in her purse when she recognizes her dad's number.

"Hey, Bran," John says in a rush. "Do you know where your mom is? Anita called and said she didn't show up for work."

"Where was she supposed to be?" Brandy counters, then learns that a local Price Chopper grocery store had expected Summer to give out food samples to customers that morning.

"Let me see what I can find out," Brandy replies, disconnecting breathlessly, and immediately heading for her mom's house. This is so unlike her mother to fail to show up for a marketing job. Summer needs the money too badly.

Brandy parks her car in the driveway, noticing Summer's car is not there. She gets out and jiggles the knob to the side door, knowing in advance it is always locked. She peeks through the glass but sees no activity. She hadn't taken the time to retrieve her set of keys to the house, so she fumes impatiently under her breath and heads back to the office, dialing her dad's number while enroute.

"Dad, why don't you meet me at Mom's? Let's see what's going on. Her car isn't in the driveway and I'm going home to get my keys."

John Shipp immediately agrees. In fact, he has already called his friend Butch Rigby to meet them there. Something tells him that having an attorney like Rigby on the scene could be a good thing. And while John knows his ex-wife can be flighty and unpredictable at times, she would never fail to show up for work. Something is definitely wrong and he can't shake the queasy unrest that has just settled in his stomach.

Even though he had found the sweetest, most wonderful woman in his second wife Naomi, John had never lost his fondness for Summer. Naomi understands and doesn't have a problem with the occasional lunches he has with Summer and Brandy.

As John parks his car in front of 3641 Pennsylvania he sees Butch pull up. Then he sees his daughter waiting at the base of the stone steps of Summer's house, keys in hand. She had sped across the Heart of America bridge, hitting speeds of 120 miles per hour in the fourth one of the Ford SHO 36-valve V-8 Tauruses she has purchased, with cash, as usual.

Brandy is almost dizzy from the quick trip she has made, but more than dizzy, she is as nervous as a cat in a room full of rocking chairs, pacing the sidewalk as she waits for John Shipp.

John gets out of his car slowly, partly from stiff muscles, but mostly from the same sense of dread his daughter is feeling. He acknowledges his longtime friend Butch, owner of the Screenland Theater, with a grim nod. They both follow Brandy as she unlocks the front door. She stands aside and lets the two men go in first. As John walks in the living room he sees an unfamiliar sight on the carpeted stairs leading to the two upper floors. Dog poop trails up almost every step. Butch sees it too and immediately takes charge of the situation, leading John and his daughter to a table in the kitchen. "You two sit here and wait until I look for Summer," he says firmly. He does not want them to find Summer in the house if something dreadful has happened to her here.

Suddenly Brandy notices the dog mess on the stairs and begins sobbing hysterically, calling for her mom's two dogs. "Alex! Miles! Come here, babies!" she calls through her tears. Here she is, acting overly emotional, just like her mom . . . something she vowed never to do. Heck, Summer even cries when her dogs get their annual vaccinations or when Brandy cuts herself peeling vegetables. She is that tender-hearted.

When the fluffy white Alex appears, the little dog is shaking and appears hesitant to approach Brandy. Miles, an older, scruffy-looking black rescue dog who is almost blind and hard of hearing, cowers in a corner of the kitchen by the back door.

"Mom would never leave these dogs by themselves," Brandy announces shakily, mentally recalling how many times Summer has taken dogs with her on her travels. Summer always stayed at Marriott hotels because she could take advantage of Brandy's associate rate of $39 (available because of her longtime stint as a bartender at the chain) but she also paid $75 extra for the animals.

It isn't long before Butch returns after searching every room on the three floors of the house. Frankly, he is relieved when he doesn't find Summer. As he comes downstairs he finds Brandy absent-mindedly stroking the fur of both Summer's dogs and John staring glassy-eyed at a seam on the retro Formica table. Suddenly, John looks up at Butch and comes alive with sudden energy. He kicks into leadership mode and starts barking orders.

"Butch, can you call the police and report a missing person? I'm going to start calling around to hospitals. Brandy, I want you to go up into your mom's office and start trying to figure out where she is working this week. Then see if you can call some of her friends who might know where she could be."

It isn't long before the house on Pennsylvania begins to bustle with activity. Someone cleans up the dog poop and one of the student boarders comes in from the UMKC library where he has been studying and volunteers to walk the dogs, relieving Brandy's guilt over those poor creatures who seem so lost and afraid. She heads upstairs and begins making calls, combing through Summer's Rolodex to determine what marketing firms she has been working for recently. On a Friday, it is hard to find anyone in the marketing firm offices, but she finally finds a wall calendar with a few items penciled in, including Susan Lawrence's party that very night. Brandy finally makes contact with a co-worker at the marketing company in New York, asks what her mother's territory would have been on Dec. 8 and 9, and then asks the friendly co-worker to fax a map of that area to Brandy's work fax. Then the distraught daughter races back to the Iron Workers office to retrieve the faxed map.

Butch had managed to call the Kansas City Police Department before Brandy gets on the extension phone upstairs. While the desk clerk has warned Butch that 24 hours have to pass before they can officially declare Summer a missing person, Brandy soon discovers it has actually been three days since she has last spoken to her mother. But the department refuses to send an officer to Summer's house. Meanwhile, John manages to squeeze in a few calls to local hospitals, with no success in finding Summer Shipp on a patient list.

Later, when Brandy comes back with the faxed map, she calls the Independence Police Department, since that's where her mother is supposed to have been working. She is also told that no report can be taken because Summer is an adult, but the desk clerk tells her she will alert officers and if anyone sees her, they will tell her that her family is concerned. Later Brandy will learn that this grim practice of treating missing persons cases of adults with 24 hour waits and outright dismissals is never due to any written rule anywhere in any police code. It is just a common practice of understaffed departments with little advanced training in missing persons cases.

John takes his now nearly hysterical daughter by the hand and leads her back to the kitchen table. From his years in the film industry and from working with public relations people, John Shipp has collected a vast network of contacts. He is going to put some of them to work now. He had called all four major television stations in Kansas City while Brandy was picking up the map. He gives addresses and contact names to his daughter. Immediately she and another family friend, Mike Heft, frantically drive to each one of the television stations to be interviewed. When the 6 and 10 o'clock news airs that night, Summer's picture and news of her disappearance will run as a lead story on all four local stations.

Brandy Shipp's striking good looks, vibrant personality, and photos of her mother are about to become familiar features to Kansas Citians, made so by the urgent desperation of family and friends determined to find the woman they adored and solve the mystery of her disappearance.

Chapter 7 – The Bronze BMW

December 11, 2004

Connie Gauger immediately rushes to her friend Brandy's side Friday night to offer her help after watching the news reports. She doesn't know Summer that well, but at 1 a.m. Brandy and Connie solidify their own 20-year friendship considerably as they drive to the closest Kinko's, one that is open all night, to begin making copies of flyers.

By Saturday morning, December 11, several dozen of Summer's friends have shown up at 3641 Pennsylvania to offer help with the search. Connie hands out flyers and the volunteers get busy tacking them up on utility poles in the area and distributing them to local businesses. Connie, who has spent all night awake with Brandy, runs to the nearest Walmart store and spends $340 for toilet paper, a coffee maker, paper plates and paper towels. When she returns to Summer's house, she counts at least 80 people coming in and out of the house, picking up flyers and asking for the latest information.

From that weekend on, Connie will canvass neighborhood eateries with flyers and ask for food donations for the army of volunteers who will work around the clock in a quest for clues. Most of the restaurants are spots that Brandy and Summer frequent and the owners or managers all happily donate food and supplies to feed the volunteers.

Searching for Summer

On Saturday a group of some 40 grim-faced volunteers fan out in the vicinity of West College Terrace in Independence. They had just completed a "staging" at Summer Shipp's house some 15 miles away in Kansas City, where an impassioned and emotional Brandy Shipp had given them the mission of finding her mom's bronze BMW. She knew from talking to her mother's bosses and marketing colleagues that Summer had been assigned to this area in Independence the day she disappeared. Meanwhile, some of the volunteers search other areas, including Parkville, where Summer had a booth in an antique mall. They even search several of Summer's favorite coffee shop hangouts and drive the areas repeatedly.

Most of those first friends who showed up over the weekend are now on the scene and ready to translate their worry into some kind of physical activity, despite the December chill. Connie and a friend named Barb have already been cruising in this neighborhood the night before. The two women had been looking for the BMW and noticed a car that matched its description. However, the license plate number that Brandy had found on a receipt in her mother's office didn't match the plate on the car they saw.

Connie now joins Brandy and the other volunteers at the intersection of North Forest Avenue and West College Terrace. They have come dressed for the cold, some with steaming cups of coffee, and all of them talk in hushed tones, waiting for instructions from Brandy and her dad. Brandy raises her arms for quiet, then directs some of them to go door to door on Forest while she and a few others plan to canvass College.

Scotti and Linda are the first to spot the BMW. They call Brandy immediately. As she begins climbing the hill on West College she notices a police car parked next to her mom's bronze BMW. Brandy heads into the wind, her red hair and wool scarf flying behind her as she runs, yelling, "Stop! That's my mom's car!"

Winded, she approaches a police officer just as he slaps a third ticket on the windshield of the aging vehicle that had been transporting Summer to all her marketing gigs (when it wasn't in the shop for repairs.) As Brandy holds her aching side, she asks the officer breathlessly, "What are you doing? This is my mother's car. She's disappeared and we know she was working in this neighborhood."

The officer seems shocked as he replies, "Ma'am, I was just about to have this car towed. It's been parked here for days and the neighbors called in a report."

"This is my mom's!" Brandy repeats, tears now streaming down her face. "We've turned in a missing persons report to the Kansas City Police Department. That was Friday night. Haven't you seen the news about Summer Shipp?" she demands, her words tumbling over each other in a flood of emotions.

"Okay! Okay! Ma'am, just calm down!" the officer replies. "Let me call this in. You'll probably need to file a missing persons report with our department if this is her car and if she was working here when she disappeared. What day was that?" he asks, flicking on his shoulder radio. He contacts the dispatcher, then asks Brandy if she has the keys to her mother's car. By then Brandy and some of her mother's friends have circled the car, trying the door handles and peering inside. They have spotted Summer's inevitable Starbucks styrofoam cup on the dash and can see personal items that they know belong to their friend.

The area around the car turns into a crime scene as yellow police tape goes up and things turn chaotic with all the searchers converging on the street. Brandy spends the next few hours in the back of an Independence police cruiser trying to stay warm and talking to the officer about her mother. The rest of the day finds her at the police department answering the same questions about Summer's disappearance that she had already covered with the officer and the Kansas City Police Department. Her frustrations are just beginning.

* * * * *

Back in his cozy home in the Waldo neighborhood of South Kansas City, John Shipp rubs his bands together in an attempt to warm up. The cold has penetrated the gloves he had worn for this morning's search. Even a lengthy visit at the Independence Police Department after they had found Summer's car has failed to thaw them out. He and Brandy had to file a second missing persons report, since it appeared Summer had gone missing in Independence instead of Kansas City. They had talked to the receptionist at the IPD, then a detective, and finally the head of the department. All the police officers had questioned them at length, zeroing in on any family members or friends that Summer might have had recent contact with or disputes with. They asked about Summer's possible drug or alcohol use, even about her sexual behavior and anyone she was currently dating. They suggested the possibility she just might have decided to purposely disappear, which caused the father-daughter duo to bristle. They both assured the officers Summer was not that kind of woman. She loved life way too much and would never leave her daughter or her beloved dogs, let alone her wide circle of friends.

Brandy and John soon realize the search for Summer will be complicated by a police department that is understaffed and already heavily involved in the search for the two Porter children, Sam and Lindsey. The youngsters had disappeared after a visit with their father and had already been missing for weeks. What an irony that two such gut-wrenching missing persons cases had fallen on the same department.

John sighs with discouragement as he feels Naomi's reassuring hands rubbing his shoulders. She places a cup of warm tea in front of him as a tear escapes and rolls down his cheek, but he sniffs and shakes himself to dispel the heaviness in his heart. He has to be strong for Brandy. Stronger than he had been last night on the phone with his sister Fran in Florida. He had called her to report Summer's disappearance and got so choked up that he handed the phone to Naomi, who filled in her sister-in-law with the rest of this unfolding story.

Just remembering that his sister is soon to arrive in Kansas City fills John with renewed optimism. Fran has a way of making everything all right. She will help them all wade through this ordeal.

* * * * *

Malisa Jennings comes out of the back room at Nick's to find two men standing at the bar. She knows they aren't regular customers. She guesses that they might be cops out of uniform. They are, and the Independence detectives have a few questions for the petite bartender. They have received several credible tips in the missing persons case they are working and came to Nick's to check them out. The tips have led them to an Independence man with several priors, and to his neighbor. Both men claim to have been in this bar at the time a woman named Summer Shipp had disappeared in their neighborhood, the place where her abandoned car had been found.

The detectives show Malisa a photo of a man. It's the man with the empty eyes. She hears them repeat the name she had already heard from the man himself–Jeffery Sauerbry. She shudders involuntarily, just like she had the two times that man had come into Nick's. She confirms for the Independence detectives that he had been in the bar that day, the day Summer Shipp disappeared.

On later reflection, something tells the tiny blonde woman that she might have just given a killer an alibi.

B 6   www.kansascity.com ★

METROPOLITAN

THE KANSAS CITY STAR.
Sunday, December 12, 2004

Police search for KC woman

By JOHN SHULTZ
The Kansas City Star

Police on Saturday were investigating the disappearance of a 54-year-old Kansas City woman who was last seen headed to her door-to-door market research job Wednesday.

Summer Shipp's family last spoke with her on Monday. On Friday, Shipp's daughter, Brandy Shipp, went to her mother's house near 36th Street and Pennsylvania Avenue and found that the dog hadn't been let out in days.

On Saturday afternoon, Independence police found Shipp's car, a bronze four-door BMW,

Summer Shipp

parked in the 1500 block of West College Terrace. Investigators checked the car and its trunk, police said. Kansas City detectives also looked at the car Saturday.

The car was found in an area where Summer Shipp was scheduled to do door-to-door work, Brandy Shipp said.

"I'm freaking out," she said. "She's perfectly healthy ... she's happy, vivacious and energetic."

Brandy Shipp said her mother

was last seen Wednesday by a foreign exchange student who lives in the same building.

One of Shipp's employers contacted the family after the woman failed to come to work Thursday or Friday.

Shipp's family on Saturday canvassed the area in Independence where she had been scheduled to work, handing out fliers and talking with neighbors.

Shipp is 5 feet 1 inch tall and weighs 105 pounds. She has strawberry-blond hair.

To reach John Shultz, call (816) 234-4427 or send e-mail to jshultz@kcstar.com.

Photo of clipping reproduced by permission of The Kansas City Star

Chapter 8 – Aunt Fran Arrives

December 15, 2004

Fran Nelson has a few hours to kill on her Delta flight to Kansas City. Thankfully, as a former employee of the airline, she was able to get a standby seat just two days after John called about Summer's disappearance. She had been in Orlando at a Red Hat event that day and couldn't get away until after the convention wrapped up, but on Tuesday she returned to Tampa and started packing.

Husband Bob urged her to go and not worry about Christmas or things at home. He'd handle it.

Fran tries to read one of the in-flight magazines, but nothing holds her attention. Soon she feels her eyes go out of focus as she stares at a poster on the forward cabin wall.

Memories come flooding back. She smiles at the recollection of how Summer Shipp had been "just a kid" when Brandy was born in 1971. The new mother doted on her precious daughter so much that all the Shipps whispered about what a brat Brandy was, due to her parents' indulgences. They still laugh about it, and even Brandy used to joke to her friends that her mother loved her so much she would probably say, "Brandy is so great. No matter that she went and robbed a bank and shot five pregnant women!"

Fran chuckles as she remembers John and Summer's philosophy of child-rearing. They wanted Brandy to be free to be creative and express herself. And so, they had installed a gym in their posh house at 54th and Holmes, near the University of Missouri-Kansas City. Summer even took gymnastics with Brandy and then supervised her practices in the home gym, as Fran remembers. Brandy also took tap and ballet lessons. And of course the huge backyard pool became the gathering place for all the kids in the neighborhood.

Despite being a spoiled brat as a child, Fran finds Brandy to be sweet and loving as an adult. For several years there were lots of little Shipp cousins at family gatherings and Brandy was so good with the younger ones.

After Summer and John divorced, Fran watched a gradual change in Brandy. She soon seemed to be the adult during her adolescence as her mother struggled to forge a new life without a husband. It wasn't long before there were lots of men coming by the houses the mother and daughter shared. And Brandy had been the one to stay up late waiting for her mother to come home from dates.

Yet through the apparent role reversal, a wild and reckless side that Fran admits may have stemmed from the dysfunctional Shipp family's history of alcoholism, showed itself in the young redhead. Brandy had become a bit of a rock band groupie, sneaking backstage after several concerts to meet the performers. Many times she even crawled on top of a dumpster and through a window at the Uptown Theater in order to go backstage to meet celebrity groups like The Red Hot Chili Peppers, Faith No More, Beastie Boys and several others. She later reported to her Aunt Fran about the fun day she had with actor Matt Dillon while he was filming a movie in Lawrence, Kansas in 1987. The celebrity worship had resulted in Brandy inviting two of the Red Hot Chili Peppers to the house on Pennsylvania when Summer was out of town. But by far the most dramatic stunt she ever pulled was leaving a note on the kitchen counter telling her mom that she was going to St. Louis to hang out with The Beastie Boys. John and Summer had anxiously awaited Brandy's return so they could have a family conference about the reckless behavior.

Young Brandy (right) and a friend Alycia Daniels with actor Matt Dillon while he was in the area filming "Kansas."

Brandy had really turned out pretty well after all this, reflects Fran. The day after she had graduated in 1988 from Bishop Miege, a Catholic high school, the 16-year-old had landed a full-time and a part-time job and had morphed into a workaholic with a strong drive to maximize her earnings. She didn't ever want to worry about money the way her mother had after the divorce.

Then Fran remembers what Brandy had later referred to as "a little tiny marriage" in Vegas one Valentine's Day. Much to her surprise, the man she wed had been smuggling drugs in from Mexico. So Brandy began flying to Arizona two or three times a month while he was incarcerated in Winslow, until she decided maybe he wasn't so good for her and divorced him quietly, even before they'd been married a year.

After that, Brandy had funneled all her energies into her three jobs. But now her mother is missing. What is the poor child going to do, Fran wonders.

As the captain announces their descent into Kansas City, she predicts her niece will somehow rise to the occasion and commit herself wholeheartedly to organizing the search for Summer. If her former sister-in-law is alive, Fran has no doubt Brandy will find her and bring her home. The girl has guts and determination to go along with her auburn-haired beauty.

As the jet taxies to the gate at Mid-Continent International, Fran sighs and stands up to reach her carry-on, even before the captain has turned off the seatbelt sign. She whispers a quick prayer, asking for a miracle.

John Shipp carries his sister's heaviest suitcase into Summer's foyer, bringing in a rush of frigid air as he follows Fran inside. Fran pauses just a moment to take in the strangers hanging over chairs and camped out on the stairs leading to her sister-in-law's upper stories. Suddenly she spies a familiar mop of red hair and sees her niece holding a phone to her head with one hand while she cups a huge coffee mug with the other, managing to dangle a lit cigarette from fingers curled around the cup.

Brandy senses her aunt's presence behind her, turns and lets out a squeal of delighted recognition. "My Aunt Fran just arrived from Florida, so I need to go. I'll try to keep you posted if we have any news," she says into the phone, barely managing to get it back on its cradle before rushing to give Fran a ferocious hug.

The emotions that Brandy had been holding in for the last several days finally give way to a torrent of sobs. Here is a motherly figure she can hold onto...someone besides her father who knows her, forgives her for all her faults and just loves her. Now she can stop putting on a brave face for the TV cameras and all the people who show up on Summer's doorstep every day wanting to help with the search. With Aunt Fran, she can be a little girl again and admit without words she is scared as hell and worried sick. Aunt Frannie will make all the hurt better and take charge, just like she had when Brandy was eight, had a bicycle wreck and skinned her knee. She had run to her aunt then because Summer had come unglued at the sight of her precious daughter bleeding.

"Hey everybody! I want you to meet my Aunt Fran," Brandy announces to the dozen people in Summer's living room. It won't be long before the search party members and all of Summer's friends adopt this tall woman with a kind face and also call her Aunt Fran.

After her luggage is deposited in a cold room on the third floor, which was to become her home for the next several weeks, Fran Nelson bustles into the kitchen, starts rummaging through cabinets and looking through the food that has appeared in Summer's refrigerator and starts a pot of "perpetual" soup that will refresh this new family of searchers and friends.

That night in an unfamiliar bed, far from her comfortable, warm home in Florida, Fran struggles to fall into an exhausted sleep. It was only when Brandy jumped in bed beside her, along with her adorable Australian Shepherd, that Fran begins to feel drowsy. She lulls herself and Brandy to sleep, telling her niece stories from her childhood and giving her a beautiful vision of the guardian angel painting Fran had hanging in her home. It depicts two children on a bridge protected by the angel's mighty wings.

* * * * *

Fran's eyes flutter open to bright sunlight streaming through the third floor window. Then the harsh reality hits her. This is no dream. Her former sister-in-law is missing and Fran has to keep Brandy's hopes up. Fran will need all her focus and strength to get through this ordeal.

Her niece is towering over her, eyes rimmed with red and hair an impossible tangle. But Fran takes comfort in hearing Brandy repeat words that Fran and Summer had chanted to Brandy as a child, "Wakey, wakey! Time to bakey! Daylight's a burnin'!" When Fran can't seem to make her body move, Brandy almost shouts, "WAKE UP! WE GOTTA FIND MY MOM!"

She summons all her optimism then, smiles a greeting at Brandy and gets ready to take a leadership role in this motherless household. They just have to find Summer Shipp and make life normal again for all of them. Summer's disappearance is just not something that happens to regular people like the Shipps. Fran has to do everything in her power to make this nightmare go away.

* * * * *

Malisa Jennings is in Independence visiting her friend, Tammy. She has just stepped onto the wooden porch and raised her fist to knock on the door when she hears her name called. She turns around to find the man with the empty eyes at her elbow.

The McDonald's Happy Meal she has just bought for Tammy's little boy dangles limply from her left hand as she stares open-mouthed at the man who has just materialized behind her. He has a Best Buy uniform on, but those eyes are the same. She would recognize them anywhere. They have been burning into her sleep for some reason, haunting her, taunting her.

"Do you remember me?" he asks softly.

She nods her head in the affirmative but her throat is so dry she doesn't trust herself to speak.

"I wanted to thank you," he says and reaches out to shake her hand. "I wanted to thank you for whatever you said to those detectives."

Malisa's heart jumps into her throat and nausea follows quickly. She doesn't answer Jeffrey Sauerbry but quickly enters the house when Tammy appears in the doorway. She tries to shut the man and his empty eyes out of her world, not yet realizing this is just the beginning of her torture.

Brandy Shipp holds one of the hundreds of "Missing" flyers searchers posted all over Independence and Kansas City in the early days of her mother's disappearance.

© The Independence Examiner, 2005, Used with permission.

Chapter 9 - Jeffrey Chace and the Chase After Clues

December 2004 into January 2005

Aunt Fran was not the only important person in Brandy's life to rush to her aid that December.

In the mid-1990s Brandy had continually bumped into Jeffrey Chace at the New Yorker Suites apartments on Baltimore Avenue. He lived on the seventh floor and Brandy lived on the eighth. He ran the valet parking service for the Italian Gardens Restaurant next door and Brandy frequently came into the well-known Kansas City eatery as the two became better acquainted.

One day Jeffrey went to Brandy's apartment to see if she was home. When she invited him in, she introduced her mother. Summer Shipp stood in the living room wearing a breezy, white chiffon dress with matching hat, glowing in the sunshine from the apartment windows. That vision, from the only time he met Brandy's mother, remains etched in Jeffrey's memory. He saw Summer as "the very definition of summer itself."

Brandy's friendship with Chace lapsed for awhile when all the residents had to move out of the New Yorker Suites, as it was sold to the Radisson Hotel chain. She moved north of the river and he moved to Columbus Park, still downtown. That is, until he took a job in Texas that enabled him to put his university computer science background to work. He began his Texas life chapter in 1997.

The telecommunications company he worked for soon sent him to The Netherlands, but once a year Chace returned to visit his family in Kansas City. He also sought the company of Brandy Shipp and they maintained their friendship.

During these annual visits, Jeffrey always invited Brandy to come and visit him in the Netherlands to enjoy exploring Europe. In 2004, Brandy accepted the invitation. During that visit the couple decided their relationship had become more than just a friendship. They made plans for his next trip in December of that year, with an agreement to meet in Boston, travel to New York, then fly back to Kansas City for the holidays.

Four days before he was to board his flight to Boston Jeffrey Chace received a frantic email from Brandy asking him to call her immediately. When they connected, Jeffrey learned that Summer had been missing since December 8. Brandy apologized but said she would not be able to meet him in Boston. Jeffrey agreed to fly to Kansas City from Boston as soon as possible. He later recalled his visit during that intense time . . .

My homecoming was naturally mixed. After having not seen her for a couple of months, I was glad to be back with Brandy in Kansas City for the Christmas holidays. But, of course the occasion was understandably overshadowed by the mystery of her mother's ill-starred disappearance.

A makeshift headquarters had been established at Summer's home, a large, old three-story house with a porch swing and stone foundations. It sat up on a rising ridge that ran through Valentine, providing the houses on Summer's side of the street with a commanding view down Pennsylvania Avenue. As a house, the old place was in need of some serious repairs and renovations. But, as a home, it was splendid –a big, warm, comfortable space exhibiting evidence of Summer everywhere. Many the night during that melancholy holiday season we sat out on the porch swing drinking, talking and wondering. Where was Summer?

The house was constantly filled with friends, family, news crews, police, everyone with the same quest– finding Summer Shipp. Her eclectic history, including having owned and run the Bijou Cinema in the Westport entertainment district, had surrounded Summer with a curious slew of interesting friends, all eager to find her, and in their intensity, there was never a still moment in those first days. The house was continuously jumping with various characters, all well-meaning, all concerned. But for Brandy, this overwhelming support, so essential at the beginning, soon became a burden. Brandy wavered between gratitude for the attention from her mother's friends and a keen desire for some peace and quiet, to be alone with her thoughts from time to time in a silent house where she could sit and ponder.

Still, that's not to say she wanted to be alone; on the contrary. Brandy wanted, and needed, the support of those closest to her. Her father, John Shipp, was a consistent presence, advising her, encouraging her, speaking to the press when needed, and lending his unconditional support. John was a rock during that turbulent time. His sister, Aunt Fran, had come up from Florida and moved into Summer's house to give Brandy additional support, with both a feminine and a cool-headed perspective. And, of course I was there.

 It was a somber Christmas for the Shipp family, but my family also lives in Kansas City and I split my time between Brandy's mom's house and my parents' place in Gladstone. From either location, we all watched the nightly news reports following Summer's case.

 One of the key characters in those early days was John Underhill, a private investigator who had read about Summer's disappearance in the local newspapers and offered his services to Brandy free of charge.

 At first, I didn't understand why Underhill would be willing to do this, but as time went on, I found him to be a caring man with good intentions who really wanted to make a difference. John Underhill was new to Kansas City, a former police detective having just moved in from Los Angeles, California, and I think that he also wanted to make a name for himself in his new city, establishing himself as a high-profile PI. Surely, he hoped to gain new business from his involvement in the Summer Shipp case, but his heart was right. John Underhill was also a constant presence in those early days.

Private Investigator John Underhill. ©Carey Media LLC, Volume 24, Number 44 issue of The Pitch, used with permission

* * * * *

 As 2004 winds down, the Shipp family and friends begin an intense schedule of events and publicity:

 December 18, 2004: Fundraiser at Harling's Upstairs. Local musicians perform in a fundraiser for the Summer Shipp Reward Fund, beginning at 2:30 p.m. Mama Ray is among the performers.

 December 19, 2004: Summer Shipp's family and friends hold a candlelight vigil in Independence at the site where her car was found. Move Up President Alvin Brooks and other Kansas City and Independence officials join the Shipp family and friends.

 December 20, 2004: Two billboards, five Kansas City Metro buses and 30 taxi-cab tops are promised to the Summer Shipp search effort. The billboards are on Southbound I-35 right before the 27th and Broadway exit and on I-435 near the Truman Road exit.

December 22, 2004: The Shipps schedule a press conference at Summer's home. Brandy Shipp tells media all she wants for Christmas is the safe return of her mother. "We're doing everything we can to get her back before the holidays," she says. Friends have decorated the house with fuschia and yellow ribbons, hoping to welcome Summer home. The reward amount increases from $35,000 to $50,000.

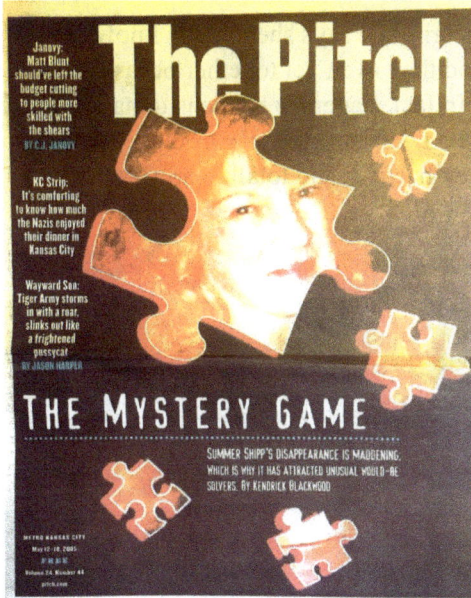

December 24, 2004: In the Valentine neighborhood where Summer lives residents gather every Christmas Eve to line the streets with candles and spend a few minutes visiting with each other. This year the luminary lighting was dedicated to Summer's safe return.

©Carey Media LLC, Volume 24, Number 44 issue of The Pitch, cover image used with permission

* * * * *

A week after a visit with Tammy and the delivery of the Happy Meal to her son, Malisa Jennings finds herself once more on her friend's front porch. And once again she hears someone call her name. This time Jeffery Sauerbry is in the side yard of Tammy's house.

"You saved my life," he says without preamble, as if to excuse his apparent stalking of her. Malisa again begins shaking but tries to downplay the role she has unwittingly filled in this mysterious missing persons case.

The fewer words she exchanges with this man, the better, so she quickly dismisses doing anything in the matter. Still, when Malisa finally gets inside Tammy's house, she is again shaking uncontrollably. This is her fourth encounter with this man! Now she doesn't know when or where he'll pop up. This is far too close for comfort.

As Tammy shut the door behind her, Malisa starts babbling almost incoherently.

"Please . . . don't ever let that man on your property! He keeps showing up at my elbow every time I'm here. I don't like his eyes. He's scary. Don't trust him and don't ever let him in the house. I think he may have had something to do with the disappearance of that woman, Summer Shipp."

Tammy laughs at Malisa's concerns and says she already knows Jeffery. Her husband knows him and they even get together occasionally for cookouts in the neighborhood. In fact, Sauerbry happens to have a good friend who lives across the street, next door to Malisa's brother-in-law. Tammy tells Malisa she finds Jeffrey friendly and totally harmless.

Chapter 10 - Psychics, Searches and Interviews

2005

Melody Gerow had been working on assignment in New York for several months. Despite her heavy responsibilities at her venue in Madison Square Garden, she could not shake a bizarre anxiety that told her to get home immediately. She took the next flight out to Kansas City. When she got home she discovered her children were fine, so there was no cause for anxiety on the home front. But she turned on the news and learned that Summer Shipp was missing.

Discovering that her best friend and first employee's mother was missing caused her to drive to Summer's house and offer her help. While she and Brandy had not been in touch much lately, the two women had an affinity that began the minute Melody interviewed Brandy for a job at her company, Locators Incorporated, in Shawnee, Kansas. That interview led to Brandy helping Melody find locations in the area to place vending machines. Eventually Brandy had her own profitable vending machine route and followed Melody in taking over several positions she would vacate in her career moves.

When Melody arrived at the Pennsylvania Avenue house that was full of anxious friends, she took Brandy aside and began coaching her for the numerous television interviews she would be appearing in. The two women practiced, filmed and replayed mock interviews to polish Brandy's on-screen persona before numerous appearances, including the Montel Williams Show. She would even travel with Brandy to Wilmington, NC to attend a few annual vigils of the CUE Center for Missing Persons.

* * * * *

The proverbial camel's back has just been fractured. And Malisa feels like the straw that has done it. Now she has to do something or she'll go nuts.

She has just arrived at Tammy's house again and who opens the door to greet her? Jeffrey Sauerbry! He grins, but those dark eyes do not grin with the mouth. They reflect only satanic emptiness as he motions for her to come inside. He walks off the porch without a backwards glance, humming some idiotic tune under his breath that could be titled, "Gotcha!"

"Now I've endangered these people," Malisa tells herself. "He can talk Tammy into letting him in," Malisa worries as she begins quizzing her friend. Once again, Tammy seems nonchalant and not at all worried about the man who has just let himself out of her house.

"He's a friend. He's a neighbor," Tammy explains once again with a dismissive toss of her head.

Malisa knows better. She knows what he was conveying when he opened the door to her knock. He had probably even overhead her frantic plea to Tammy to keep him away the last time she had visited.

What Malisa will not tell Tammy is that her dreams are now haunted by Summer Shipp. In the recurring dream scene Malisa is on a boat dock that has some loose boards. She lifts up a board and sees Summer's upturned face in the water. Summer pleads, "Hurry!"

Each time the dream returns, Summer's face appears more hazy, more distorted, more decayed from being in the water. And her cries become fainter. Malisa knows it is time to try to communicate with the Shipp family.

When she gets home, still shaken from her latest encounter with Jeffery Sauerbry, she boots up her computer and types "friendsofsummer.com" into the address bar on her browser.

* * * * *

Kris Wade had heard that her good friend, Summer Shipp, was missing when someone called to ask if she had seen her lately. She hadn't, at least not since Thanksgiving when Kris went to Summer's to hang out. The two women had been introduced through mutual friend Connie Vitale, who owned Autographs in Crown Center, and later Love Records in Westport. They immediately became inseparable, going shopping together, to plays, movies and brunches in Summer's back yard. One of their favorite activities was to just sit and talk on the swings at Roanoke Park.

With dread in her heart, Kris immediately went to Summer's house to offer her assistance. She was working on a criminology and criminal justice degree at the University of Missouri-Kansas City at the time. That course work and her advocacy work with Kansas City's "women of the night" caused her to immediately think the worst about Summer's disappearance. In fact, almost right away the girls who worked Independence Avenue began calling her about a man named Jeffery Sauerbry. Of course, they would never have called police, but instead reported to Kris with stories like, "He hog-tied me and wouldn't let me go." He was already known to police and was on parole for a federal weapons charge. The women told Kris he was famous for stalking and the word on the streets was that he had killed Summer Shipp. They also reported Sauerbry was possibly connected to the murder of a William Kellett, a security guard at an Independence used car lot, back in 1998.

Kris's contacts with the prostitutes and her degree work gave her some credibility with the Independence Police, so she quickly became an informal liaison and an advocate for Brandy in some of the family's conferences with detectives. She also developed a rapport with PI Underhill.

Kris gained even more respect for the private investigator the day he organized a massive volunteer search of an area near William Chrisman High School in Independence. Police had already searched the area with dogs but had found nothing. Underhill organized a shoulder-to-shoulder search of the same area on a cold day in February of 2005.

During the search, one of the volunteers had kicked a piece of plastic with her shoe. It turned out to be a Sutherlands Friends and Family Card issued to Summer Shipp.

Underhill handed the card to police officers. In what was later termed a knee-jerk reaction, one of the officers accused Underhill of planting the card. Eventually, the adversarial relationship between the PI and the Independence Police Department led to the former's departure. Underhill felt he was no longer able to be effective in the search for Summer.

Kris felt the police did the best they could. But so did Underhill. From her course work at UMKC she already knew police needed a probable cause to arrest someone, which is a high standard. Plus, they have to go through a lot of formalities before they can even execute a search warrant. Yet the department didn't give up.

Kris and others involved in the search wanted desperately to go into Jeffrey Sauerbry's back yard. After all, he had a big pit dug back there and they wanted to be sure Summer hadn't been or wasn't in that pit. They even tried to spy on the yard from the vantage point of one of Sauerbry's neighbors' houses. But according to the neighbor, Jeffrey quickly began stalking her in the same way he stalked the prostitutes on Independence Avenue. He had apparently formed his own suspicions one evening when he caught Kris, a friend and the neighbor looking at his property from the neighbor's yard. He immediately came into the neighbor's yard and afterwards began a campaign to intimidate her.

Besides helping with the searches and being a go-between with police, Kris Wade wrote a letter to Nancy Grace that led to Brandy appearing three times on her nationally syndicated television news show. Brandy would ultimately also appear on the Montel Williams Show and America's Most Wanted.

* * * * *

Thanks to a friend of Summer's with web design expertise, a website called *Friends of Summer* began to serve as a hub for event notifications and fundraising efforts, helping to quickly disseminate information and solicit tips in the continuing search. If anyone wanted to reach Brandy, they could do so without trying to obtain her phone number. And many people did use the website. Yet checks to help with the reward fund that Brandy set up usually came in the mail or were brought by Summer's house with heartfelt notes or letters attached, such as the one from Sue Herrick.

January 8, 2005

Dear Brandy,

It was so nice talking with you again and your Aunt Fran. What a lovely lady! It must run in the family! As we talked about, please use the enclosed $1,000 check for whatever will help you most.

Am looking forward to seeing you again Thursday evening, meeting Aunt Fran and other family/friends in person.

Until then, and always, take good care.

Love and prayers,
Sue Herrick

The Friends of Summer website received voluminous information and emails in the early days. Many of them were from well-wishers and people who wanted to donate to the search fund. The website was also used to organize volunteers for searches like the one where Summer's Sutherlands card was found.

The big task facing Brandy and her loyal volunteers was how to discern legitimate tips as they weeded out the crackpots, questionable psychics and all the morbid curiousity seekers who seemed to be attracted to the case.

The name of Jeffrey Sauerbry surfaced in multiple tips. Each time it did, Brandy forwarded the messages to the Independence police.

To: Friends of Summer website
Date: Mon, May 16, 2005
 Subject: I work with Jeff Sauerbry and may have info
I am not sure what type of help this will be, but I am currently working with Jeff Sauerbry. I am a cemetery director at Mt. Washington and have been sent on several appointments with Jeff for training purposes. I am training several employees and my boss has sent me with Jeff on some visits with potential customers (for pre-need burial policies). On one occasion about a week ago, Jeff asked if I could take him to his house so that he could let his dog out. It was a very odd place and I did not stay inside for very long. However, I was in the backyard and saw the dug-out pond area. Jeff told me that he had been building a pond for his mom, but could not finish it since he could not afford more liner. I thought this was odd at the time. We were running short on time, so I asked him if he would consider door-knocking in his own neighborhood. He replied that his neighborhood was not a "good thing right now" and that the people didn't like him very much.

During the next appointment I was sent on, Jeff told me he had just gotten out of prison for having a gun, but did not go into specifics. I used to work in prison reform, so this did not alarm me immediately. He did snap at the customer during the visit because her large dogs kept sniffing him. He snapped and demanded that she put her animals outside. He did it in such a manner that it took both of us aback.

We have also discussed Summer's disappearance slightly. When I told him of the benefits of door knocking, he asked if I always went alone. I told him that, generally, I was not afraid, but things can happen. I told him that since Summer disappeared in the area we would be in, I like to take a partner. I joked and said that no one would likely mess with me if I had a big guy with me. I told him that we didn't have to live in fear, but that

Searching for Summer

Summer Shipp disappeared doing about the same job and you never know if there is a psycho that will grab you or invite you in and never let you leave. I told him that she was probably like me and would enter a home if invited, not ever thinking of the bad in people. I said that it was scary to think that someone can just disappear like that.

He sat silent during this and just said that he had never heard of the case. This took place before I read the article in the Pitch and put two and two together that I knew the suspect. His home has a stench inside of it that I cannot describe. This is why I stood outside while he got his dog on the leash. I found it odd that he said he knew nothing of a woman who disappeared doing door-knocking, yet is the prime suspect.

On the way to appointments, Jeff is always trying to get me to take side and back roads rather than main streets, yet I have refused. I always had the suspicion that he was just trying to get fresh with me. However, I am engaged and was not interested in anything of that nature, so have tried to stay as distant and professional as possible. He also calls quite a bit asking for rides to appointments and for help, etc. However, I never gave him my contact info and have asked him not to use my cell number since it is for emergency purposes. He was very angry that I chewed him out for bothering me so much.

One of our new counselors recently had her car broken into. As a seemingly good Samaritan deed, Jeff offered to help her fix the window. She agreed and he took her to a junk yard to get a window. The woman was reluctant to go, but Jeff convinced her that junk yards were not as creepy or strange as some might think, so she went.

These events are so very odd to me and the fact is: he now has a job where he is in homes quite a bit. I am fearful of this and of going to work. Feel free to contact me and I will try to help in any way possible. I am not sure what value my conversations with Jeff might hold, but I am willing to help.

Sincerely yours,
Elizabeth

The Friends of Summer website received several calls from legitimate psychics and empaths but just as many from individuals with doubtful credentials.

Date: Wed, May 25, 2005 at 2:41 PM
Subject: I would like to help
I have written before.

I am cursed with seeing things and no one believes me. However, so often I am right. I saw in my mind what happened to your mom. Maybe I am right, maybe I am wrong. I would be willing to talk with you and/or your private detective. I have contacted the Independence PD in regards to the Porter kids' case. This was the response I got: Have you ever seen a mental specialist? So why come forward to you? Because it seems all other leads have failed. And I feel really the investigation is in the total wrong direction. At least give it a shot. (Contact information redacted)

I am 62 years old and this is a lifetime thing with me, my being so right. I freak my wife out with the detail of what I see. I am sure if you just listen maybe some lights will come on. That may bring an end to this tragic chapter in your life.

Because I work and do not want fame or the limelight of the media, I do not want the people I work with to react to my being in the news. I have three children– one in the US Army in Afghanistan and two that live in Blue Springs. I have been married 41 years. So I hope this brings some credibility to my life. You may contact me through ****** as this is my other screen name and contact name to the Independence PD.

Hope I can help.
(Name redacted)

From: Deb West
To: underhill@prodigy.net
Cc: friendsofsummer@gmail.com
Sent: Tuesday, June 14, 2005 11:38 PM
Subject: neighborhood council meeting
I wanted to let you know what I heard today. I didn't get to go to the meeting because it was my daughter's birthday..but the neighbor told me Jeff and his mother showed up.They said neither of them said a word... just sat there. Then they told me another woman who lives by him is being approached in the same way we were. He asked her to come to his house to see a puppy. A guy who lives closer to me rents to her, and she told him. I told them to tell her to be careful.

Deb

Brandy began using the website herself to communicate with

supporters and volunteers. She used it for updates on the case, to notify friends of special fundraisers and to thank everyone for their continued interest.

Email from Brandy to Friends of Summer subscribers:
Subject: Six Month Anniversary
Date: June 8, 2005
Dear Friends,

The correct words seem to escape me as I try to best express my deep appreciation for all the support, concern, and heartfelt efforts which so many of you have displayed since my mother vanished without a trace.

Today marks six months from the last day my mother was seen or heard from on December 8, 2004.

I know my mother's disappearance has affected thousands of people in so many different ways and each person has their own way of dealing with the situation. But, I also know that we all share many common emotions, such as sadness, pain, and confusion. I, personally, am still living in a world of numbness. I have realized, though, that I would have been unable to function at all without the inner strength which God has given me, and also the tremendous support of those around me.

We have successfully bonded together as a community and kept my mother's story in the public eye. We must, because that is what will ultimately lead us to my mother.

I will continue, as I have been, trying to spread the word of my mom's disappearance and trying to gain more national exposure. I will also continue doing what I can to raise awareness of the issue of missing adults, because I truly believe it is one of America's most under-recognized problems.

If it takes us six more hours, six more days, six more months or six more years, we will continue to look for Summer Shipp until we find her.

Please continue to keep in touch however possible, whether it be by phone, by email, in person, or by signing the guestbook when visiting www.friendsofsummer.com.

Thank you from the bottom of my heart for all the love you have shown in so many different ways.

Please keep my mother in your thoughts and prayers.

Brandy Shipp

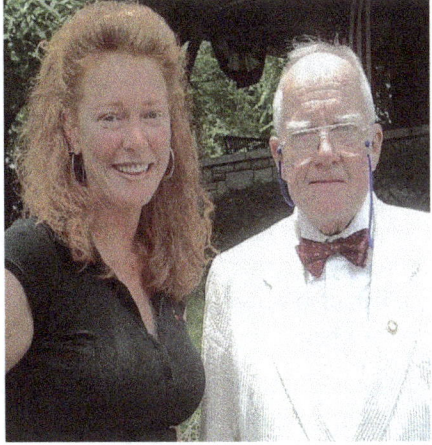

Date: Wednesday, July 6, 2005
Subject: Friends of Summer Recent and Upcoming Events
Dear Friends of Summer,

Coming up on the seventh month since my mother disappeared, the search continues in earnest even as the media has turned its attention for the time being to other stories which have captured the public's attention. My heart goes out to the many families such as the Holloways (whose daughter Natalie disappeared while on a spring break trip to Aruba) who are experiencing the same sorrow and sense of loss which I have known all too well.

Although there is not much to report at this time as to developments, clues or breakthroughs in our ongoing investigation, I would like to inform you of a unique opportunity that literally came to my doorstep yesterday as

our nation was celebrating Independence Day. The Valentine Neighborhood Association held its annual Fourth of July Parade and since my mother's house is in Valentine, the parade proceeded right in front of her house.

Former Kansas City Mayors–Congressman Emanuel Cleaver and State Senator Charles B. Wheeler–and City Councilman Jim Glover were dignitaries for the celebrations. I was able to talk with Congressman Cleaver right outside of my mother's house and update him on the status of her case. After the parade Senator Wheeler took a moment to talk with me and also offered to meet to discuss the case and determine what can be done to help.

I am continuing to do what I can to keep people aware of my mother's story and to do what I can to help others who are missing loved ones. I have been making commitments to speak at vigils for other missing persons. On May 25, 2005, I traveled to Wilmington, NC as a guest at the Cue Center's 11th Annual Waterfront Vigil. Also, on July 16, I will be traveling to Beaumont, Texas to speak at a vigil for Kimberly Langwell, who has been missing since July 9, 1999.

Thank you for continuing to support the search of Summer and for all of the efforts each one of you have provided. I will keep you updated as new developments occur.

Brandy Shipp

To: Nancy Cipolla of Kansas City Transportation Group
Date: Tuesday, Aug. 2, 2005
Nancy,

I would like to let you know how very much I appreciate your continuing to display my mother's missing posters on the tops of Yellow Cabs. It is very important to me to keep her picture and story in the public eye and it is people like you that are helping make that possible.

I often receive emails from people commenting on how great they think it is that the posters are still being displayed. I also receive phone calls from people who tell me they are sitting in traffic next to a taxi-cab and looking at Summer Shipp's picture.

Anyhow, I just wanted to pass that along. Your support is very much appreciated by many people and does not go unnoticed.

Brandy Shipp

Then, in the heat of the summer, and among the many notes of support, two more messages about Jeffrey Sauerbry come in. Malisa Jennings has finally found the courage to act in spite of (or perhaps because of) her fears for her own safety.

From: Malisa
Tuesday August 9, 2005
Subject: PLEASE READ THIS, I MAY KNOW SOMETHING THAT CAN HELP
Dear Brandy,

My name is Malisa Jennings, and I hope to possibly have some information that may help with the investigation of Summer's disappearance. I have already talked to Detective Christiansen in the past. I was the last place of business Jeff Sauerbry was at 45 minutes prior to the disappearance of your mother Summer, I was bartending that day and served both him and his neighbor, who was the last one who saw her walk towards Jeff's house.

Today I watched a re-run of the Montel Williams show, and saw your interview. Then I went online and found the article that was written in The Pitch, and read in the article about Jeff asking the same neighbor he was at the bar with if he had any family buried at Mount Washington Cemetery. That's when I knew I had to contact you about someone else who also knows Jeff Sauerbry, who started coming in to the bar a few months after the Detective questioned me. I was unaware she or her husband knew Jeff until one night they all three showed up at that same bar, and I was paged with an urgent request to come and identify if that was the same guy police had questioned me about. By the time I arrived they had just left, but the bartender on duty described him perfectly and even said he introduced himself as Jeff. That's when I found out that he was associated with the two other customers that had just recently been frequenting the bar.

PLEASE contact me, so I can pass along the information on how to contact these other people. I think I have something very important to tell you concerning a conversation I had with the woman and her association with Mount Washington Cemetery. PLEASE, please, contact me.

Malisa Jennings

From: IndepMo.Com Police Scanner <scanner@indepmo.com>
Date: Sun, Aug 28, 2005 at 1:54 PM
Subject: Jeffrey Sauerbry Scanner Recording
I was trying to call Mr. Underhill to pass on some information I heard on the scanner this morning. A female answered and stated I had the wrong number.

I met John and another person in the woods on 24 highway after I discovered some clothing a few months back. I told him about the website I ran and he asked that if I heard anything on the scanner to pass the info on to him.

I put together a recording clip regarding Jeffrey Sauerbry this morning. If John has a new phone number, could you pass it on to me for future incidents such as this? Thanks.

Here is a breakdown of what's on the recording:

Jeffrey Sauerbry called Independence Police on 8/28/05 around 10:20 a.m. stating someone broke into his residence at 1515 W. College and tried to kill him overnight. Dispatch tells officers a short time later that he has J8 (drugs) in his stomach. Officers arrive to be greeted by a pit bull. Sauerbry was transported by ambulance to Research Medical Center with an Independence Police Officer following.

Joe, IndepMo.Com
Recorded Independence Missouri Police Scanner Incidents

It was through the website that Brandy began networking with organizations and individuals focused on missing persons cases. That networking would lead her feet-first into becoming an advocate for families of missing persons.

From: Kelly Jolkowski
To: friendsofsummer@gmail.com
Sent: Saturday, August 20, 2005 1:10 AM
Subject: Hello from Kelly
Dear Brandy,

I saw that you signed Jason's guestbook and linked him on your site for your mom. Thank you for your kindness. I feel bad in a sense because I do not have your mom posted in our forum, or anywhere else. There are so many cases, I just cannot post them all, and your mom's was just one of the ones I did not pick.

I would be very happy to feature her as a story in our Project Jason blog, if you are interested in doing that. You can see the blog by clicking on the link in my signature. Feel free to check it out and see what you think. If you want to do it, then I have a questionnaire that I would email to you. You would answer the questions, and email it back to me. I try to write missing person's stories several times per week, mixed in with educational and other related information.

At Ashley's vigil, why didn't you come up and introduce yourself to me? I would have loved to have met you and talked. I had no idea you were there, or I would have sought you out. It's not often that we get to meet family members in person.

Thank you also for your kind comments about my speech.

Kelly Jolkowski, mother of Missing Person Jason Jolkowski
President and Founder, Project Jason
www.projectjason.org

From: Friends of Summer
Date: Sat, Aug 20, 2005 at 4:58 PM
Subject: Re Summer Shipp
To: Guarding Angels
Janet,
Thank you for your quick response to my email. My mother worked for several different market research companies. Many were local, many were not. She did things like mystery shopper, movie trailer checks, focus groups, etc, etc. She did door-to-door for ONLY ONE Company, NOP World, formerly known as Roper Worldwide. That is what she was doing when she disappeared.

I was in New York City for the taping of the Montel Williams show in March 2005, so we designed a special flyer. We used my mother's missing flyer with her picture and info about her disappearance, but we added to the lower half of the flyer the following info:

NOP World (formerly Roper Worldwide) is a corporation with revenues over $350 million. Summer Shipp has been working for them for over ten years doing market research in the Kansas City metro area.

In early December 2004 she was assigned to an Independence, MO neighborhood to conduct market research surveys door-to-door. The first day she worked this designated area, December 8, 2004, she was abducted and has not been seen since. Because no specific physical evidence has come to light, she is still considered "MISSING." Family, friends and the Independence Police Department continue to work on the case, but other than initial replies to inquiries by authorities and family, NOP WORLD has not done one thing to help in the search for Summer. Family and friends want to know

WHY HAS NOP WORLD ABANDONED SUMMER SHIPP?

1. Does the management of NOP have no heart?

2. Do they have no sense of social responsibility?

3. Why have they refused to respond to the family's request for financial help on the reward and ongoing search, and help to go national?

4. Why did they ask their employees to cut off contact with Summer's family?

5. Why did they assign a single female, carrying cash, to an area with several known sexual predators?

6. Did they supply Summer with safety guides?

7. Why have they, since Summer's abduction, deleted all material relating to door-to-door research from their website?

8. Should a company take responsibility for people who work for them?

We would like some answers from NOP world!!

We believe it is wrong for a company to abandon its employees!

We then posted these special flyers on poles on the street of NOP World's office on Ninth Avenue in NYC. We plastered these posters up and down approximately 8-10 streets surrounding the NOP HOME OFFICE. They were 11" X 14" and bright yellow.

We still have not heard back from the company. And unfortunately, I am not at liberty to say much more, because further on down the road, there will be legal issues. But for now, I am focusing on finding my mother. That is what matters to me. Legal issues are not even close to being important at this time and can wait.

I think the flyer above will answer some of your questions. I will answer the rest.

Did she have to check in with anyone every so often? Just to be sure she was okay or anything?

No, she did the work on her own schedule.

Do they know the area she was last in? If so, what is the address there?

They designated the area. That is how we were able to locate her car. It was parked where she was supposed to be surveying.

Did she carry a cellphone or radio? If so, did they pick up the signal of her cellphone at all?

She had lost her cell phone a month prior and had not replaced it yet. But she did not check in with anyone anyway.

Could you just give me a little info. on the background of her job such as did she have to report to somebody first, then go to the door to door stuff, or was this something she ran from home or what? And give me a little description of any safety measures they had to keep their employees safe.

NOP WORLD would FedEx her a big packet with the survey questionnaires, screener forms, all the info needed for each particular job at a time, including the deadline for the completed surveys to be returned to NOP. Also they included a very detailed map of the areas she was to do the work.

Did she have any medical problems that might have made her confused and she walked away somewhere?

NO medical problems at all. She was of sound mind, healthy and happy with life. She would NEVER just walk away by choice.

Who is the LAST person that saw her for sure?

The police think it was a person on the block where her car was found. When she left his house, he saw her walking across the street to another house around 4:30 p.m. and she never made it back to her car.

How was she acting that day? Happy? Sad? Any different than usual?

Completely normal as she could be.

Any problems such as financial, romance, etc?

No problems other than typical life, balancing funds like most of

America. No boyfriend at the time. She would NEVER just walk away.

Please feel free to contact me anytime thru email or phone.

It would be so appreciated if you could feature her picture and a link on your homepage http://guardingangels.4ourangel.com

Thank you for your time,

Always hopeful,
Brandy Shipp

From: Friends of Summer
Date: Sat, Aug 27, 2005 at 5:04 PM
Subject: Hello from Brandy Shipp
To: Kelly Jolkowski <kelly.jolkowski@projectjason.org>
Hi Kelly,

I apologize for the delay in returning your email. Had a million things going on at once and I fell a little behind, but am now catching up.

Yes I would love for you to feature my mother's story in your Project Jason blog. Please email me the questionnaire and I will be happy to fill it out and return to you. I would appreciate it very much.

At Ashley's Vigil, I spoke to her mother when it was over, and then I did not see you around, otherwise, of course, I would have gladly introduced myself. I am very interested in being involved in any sort of events, vigils, conferences, ANYTHING that has to do with missing persons. I have flown to Beaumont, TX and Wilmington, NC to speak at other vigils and I want to continue to do things of that nature. I realize this is going to be part of the rest of my life and I want to help make a difference any way I can.

Please, please keep me posted of any upcoming activities or events. I will be looking forward to receiving the questionnaire.

Thanks again.

Always hopeful,
Brandy Shipp

From: Llrule30@aol.com
Sent: Tuesday, August 30, 2005 3:46 AM
Subject: Hi Brandy, it's Leslie Rule! (Author and daughter of the late true crime author Ann Rule)

Hi Brandy!

I think of you and your mom every day!

I will get busy thinking about media channels for you. The little girl in Utah was found because her family kept her image in the media. I can't think of her name–Samantha (Elizabeth Smart), or something like that. She's blonde and plays the harp. I'm sure you know all about it. She's the one that was found with the couple.

I have a friend, Jacque MacDonald, who has a small radio show and public TV show in California–both called "The Victim's Voice." Her daughter was a victim so she does this work to help others. If you like, I can ask her if she will interview you on her show. I'm sure she would do it. And she knows lots about the media as she used them to find her daughter's killer. She is a very nice lady and would be a great person for you to talk with. Would you like me to put you in touch with her? Though California is far away from you, it couldn't hurt for you to do a phone interview.

You might remember that Jacque was in my book COAST TO COAST GHOSTS. Her daughter's ghost made friends with a little boy.

I have an article on ghosts that will be in the November issue of Reader's Digest, out in October. I had queried them about doing an article about missing people and Jane Does last fall, but they said they'd already done something similar and asked me to write about ghosts instead. I next sent the query to PARADE magazine, but the editor misplaced it and asked me to resend it. If they, by chance, go for it and let me include missing cases, I'll push to mention your mom. In the end it would be up to the editor.

If you like, I can email you a copy of the query I sent to them but keep in mind that it includes lots of sad cases with bad endings. I wrote the query before your mom disappeared.

Leslie Rule

From: Friends of Summer
Date: Tue, Aug 30, 2005 at 1:25 PM
Subject: From Brandy Shipp
To: Llrule30@aol.com
Hi Leslie,

Yes I would love to read the query you sent Readers Digest. Please email it to me. And I will be sure to check out your article in November Readers Digest.

Also, yes, I would be happy to do a phone interview with Jacque. She can email me or call me to set up the details, etc.

Thank you so very much for everything. If you ever need a story idea for a book, feel free to consider my mother's story. I'd be happy to help in any way.

Always hopeful,
Brandy

From: Randall Nagel
Sent: Thursday, September 8, 2005
Subject: What's new?
Are there any developments noteworthy of your mother's disappearance? I look at the website weekly and notice that nothing seems to be evolving, so I was just wondering. I keep you both in my prayers daily. God Bless.

Always, Randy

From:Friends of Summer
Date: Fri, Sep 9, 2005
To: Randall Nagel
Hi Randy,

Actually, there is still a lot going on behind the scenes with the Police Department, just nothing that can be publicized. My father and I meet with the Independence detectives every Friday, usually for 1 to 1-1/2 hours. Each time The Montel Show replays, they get more leads, but, no, nothing solid. We keep thinking that something will unfold and that it is just a matter of time, and I am still trying eagerly to get more national media attention.

Soon I will have to put my mom's house on the market and sell it. Financially I just cannot continue paying two mortgages (I own a house north of the river).

Thanks for keeping in touch. It's great to hear from you. Please continue to check in. And, you ARE on the mailing list. I just haven't sent any emails out in the last few months. I am glad to hear you check the website   *Brandy*

To: friendsofsummer@gmail.com
Sent: Thursday, September 08, 2005 7:39 PM
Subject: Leslie Rule Here!

Hi Brandy!

I've been thinking of you! Do you ever watch "Psychic Detectives" on Court TV?

My friend, Nancy Myer, has been featured on there many times. I don't know if she could help or not, but if you want I can hire her for an hour or two, over the phone to see if she can come up with something. It costs one hundred an hour over the phone.

She charges $5,000 a day plus expenses to actually travel to the area and if I were rich, I'd hire her for that. I could afford to pay her for two hours over the phone, but she doesn't work directly with families–just the police. I think that it is too hard for psychics to have family there if something bad comes out.

I'm still holding onto the possibility that your mom is being held somewhere and has perhaps experienced "the Stockholm Syndrome." This is the brainwashing that Patty Hearst experienced when she was kidnapped.

Norma Jean (a former friend of Leslie's who was reportedly psychic) talked a few times to your private detective, John. I don't know if she helped at all. I have witnessed her being very accurate, but she also embellishes and I would not want her working on something so delicate.

Do you want me to hire Nancy for a couple of hours? I will donate the two hundred dollars and I could set up a three way line with your private detective or local police officer and me. I want to be in on it as I feel a psychic connection with your Mom and maybe I could help too.

It sounds like the police (as opposed to your private detective) have more clout as far as making things happen. Do you suppose if we sent them copies of some episodes of Nancy on Court TV they would be convinced to give it a try? Nancy would need a photo of your mom and maybe a personal item to hold. Maybe also photos of where she was last seen.

I met Nancy years ago when I was writing for **Woman's World** magazine and they assigned me an article on psychics who work with police to solve crimes. She claims an eighty percent accuracy, but I don't know if it is really that high. I'm sure the **Psychic Detective** episodes leave out all the parts where the psychics are wrong, but they ARE right much of the time.

I'm brainstorming as I write this, but I just got an idea. What if we got some TV show interested in bringing several well known psychics together on the case? If nothing else, it would generate media attention for your mom's plight. I have lots of media contacts, and I'd be happy to help set the wheels in motion. I can't promise anything, but we could try it.

Let me know your thoughts on all of this. What do you want me to do next?

I just can't imagine how hard this time must be for you. I want to fly there just to give you a big hug. Maybe I can sometime soon!

Love,
Leslie Rule

The communications on the website eventually settled into what might be considered the mundane, routine details of life, such as what to do with one of Summer's dogs (the other animal had to be put down due to illness and old age) and Brandy having to sell her mother's house.

From: Friends of Summer
Date: Sun, Sep 11, 2005
To: Bob Perry
Hi Bob,

So sorry I have not gotten back with you sooner. I just returned from a small vacation in Washington DC, and am SO behind (even more than usual!) in returning emails, phone calls, correspondence, etc, etc. But I am back in KC and will catch up soon enough.

I hadn't forgotten you! I want to thank you for the lovely card and pin you sent me. That was so thoughtful! And thank you for the voice mail you left me. I am glad you received the packet I sent to you. Also, how very nice it was to read the Guestbook Entry you left on my mom's site. I appreciate your kind words. I am still plugging away trying to get more national media attention on her case. I am also still so focused and dedicated in doing what I can to be involved in other missing persons events and to continue to try to raise awareness any way I can.

Well, I just wanted to touch base with you and say HI! I think I will be in Oceanside visiting my friend, Grace, during the last week of October. Hope all is well with you. Have a great day !

Brandy Shipp (your favorite bartender in Kansas City)

Date: Mon, Oct 3, 2005 at 9:33 PM
From: Jim Overman (former boyfriend of Summer's who had taken in her dog)
Sent: Monday, October 03, 2005 11:55 AM
Subject: Alex
Hey Bran,

I was hoping you could take care of Alex for me from Oct. 18-Nov.1. I'm going to be out of town. I think she would be less freaked-out if she were with you. (She's very sensitive, you know.) Can you help me out? I would be very grateful.

Jim

Hey Jim,

I would be more than happy to do so if possible. However, I am scheduled to be out of town from Oct. 20 through Oct 28. With my life the way it has been, my plans change daily. The last trip I had planned (a few weeks ago) I had to cancel because Kirina (Brandy's own dog) has had many ailments—all of a sudden—so, after 4 or 5 visits to the vet, she had to be sedated last Monday. They removed a tumor from her jaw and an abscessed tooth and cleaned the teeth, and X-RAYed her front right leg. They concluded that she has permanent nerve damage in that leg and she will be limping for life. All of a sudden I realized how my mother felt about Miles and Alex. I can sooooo relate, in the fact that I cannot leave my puppy (10 yrs old) with just anyone.

I have moved back to MY house—in Gracemore—because I have a work crew at 3641 seven days a week and I am trying to fix the house up very minimally so that I can sell it. It is being painted and being fixed up enough to be able to sell. New gutters (there were none), termites infested the southwest corner and they have now been treated. Chimney guy gave me the paperwork that states the fireplaces are unsafe for wood-burning. Anyway, to answer your question about taking care of Alex, I want to if possible. I just need to rethink my next trip, because it is very possible I may cancel it. So I would like to get back with you in the next few days.

Please let me know your thoughts on this. Alex will be a major fact in my decision, and I appreciate that you asked me to take care of her.

Brandy

Date: Thu, Dec 1, 2005
 Subject: ALEX
To: Jim Overman
Hi Jim,

Just wondering what the plans are for Alex.

I will be out of town Dec. 19 thru Dec 29, and out of town Jan 5 thru Jan 12. However, I would love to keep Alex while I am in KC. I asked my wonderful vet about boarding and the phone number is 913-287-4964. I would be happy to pick up Alex and drop her off and any other thing needed. Please let me know either way, so I can plan accordingly.

Talk soon,
Brandy

P.S. Also, I do hope you can make it to the Tribute on Dec. 8. If not, I understand.

The Tribute will mark the first anniversary of Summer's disappearance. By now, hope that she will be found alive has diminished in most people's minds. Thoughts now turn to celebrating her life by sharing memories of a delightful woman.

Chapter 11 - Fond Summer Memories

Tribute to Summer Shipp

Family and friends are joining together to celebrate our love and happy memories of Summer.

December 8, 2005

6:00 to 8:00 p.m.

Screenland Theater

1656 Washington (one block west of Broadway)

Anyone who would like to share thoughts or a great Summer story at the tribute please contact Diane. In addition, we are compiling a memory book for Brandy. If you have a written memory, photo or anything you would like to share, please email us by Dec.1 or bring it to the tribute. Anyone wishing to bring food or flowers, please contact Marg.

As always, thank you for your kind thoughts and prayers. This celebration of Summer, and all she has meant to those who have been touched by her kind nature and presence ,will be a wonderful event.

I look forward to seeing all of you. Summer's family and friends thank you for your support and efforts.

* * * * *

The tributes received at the Summer Shipp memorial event were a testament to her vibrant personality and the quality of her friendships. The following stories from her friends are the ones that Brandy and Summer's extended family would come to treasure and focus on in the years following her disappearance, rather than the gruesome details of her death that would eventually be discovered.

Searching for Summer

Oh my goodness, I have some absolutely wonderful and possibly unique stories of Summer. Like the gifts she gave me when I was just out of college. A chocolate tin full of marbles, an "Eraserhead" mask and a copy of what she said at the time was her favorite book, *Wait Until Sunrise*, by Bandini.

She was also my companion when I won a trivia contest at the Uptown Theater. I won a VHS tape of vintage Christmas cartoons which we went to her place on Pennsylvania to watch.

On one of our outings to a punk concert, Summer broke out false piercings to put in her ears and nose and was content to stand to the side while I indulged myself in the mosh pit.

In short, she was simply one of the most pure of heart and decent-minded people I've ever known.–*David Yonnally*

I have many fond, funny and lovely memories of Summer and Brandy. I love Summer so much. Last night I was sitting in my room thinking about the (tribute) party coming up Dec. 8. Missing Summer, I glanced at a shelf where sat a mime porcelain doll. That doll is the twin of another doll that is Summer's. We each saw the same doll around Christmastime of some wonderful year during our 30 year friendship and gave them as a gift to each other. --Connie Vitale

There was a girl named Summer
Who was such a good friend like no other
She was thoughtful and sweet
To all those that she'd meet ...
To not know her would be a real bummer.
–Sue Herrick

One evening I was out and about and reached into my pocket to find something that I knew very well I had not put there. When I looked back I realized I had been with Summer the last time I had worn that coat. And so I laughed out loud at this foreign object in my pocket—a condom. I can just imagine the impish grin on her face as she discreetly tucked it into my pocket. A condom! Summer's own little way of saying, "forget me not." And so I never will.**–Carolyn Wheeler**

I remember my first "Girls of Summer" dinner party in Carolyn's backyard, poolside. I knew no one except Carolyn but could tell as each of the women arrived, "I am going to like this group." Lively, outgoing,

vivacious and wild, creative dressers, they were my kind of women!

About an hour after I got there, Summer came through the door in all her radiance: huge smile, hand extended, and just the biggest hello. As the evening progressed and the margaritas flowed, Summer and I ended up poolside talking and realized we both had one daughter, the same age, and absolutely the single most important person in our lives! We talked on and on about the beauty of Brandy and her self-assured personality, and compared notes on what life had been like as Mom to only one child, and a daughter, no less.

Summer and I bonded; there was no doubt in my mind that we would be having many conversations together about Brandy and Kristie and our dreams for these beautiful young women we love so much. I can truly say I miss Summer regularly. I so wish we would have had more of those conversations back then, and I truly know in my heart that wherever Summer is Brandy is singularly the person she is powering love towards. *–Janice Kinney*

I did not know Summer personally, but I have heard of her many times from my sister, who lives right next door to her. My sister has a very annoying Beagle that used to stay out all night. Soon after my sister moved in, Summer left her a very nice note with flowers on it that suggested she leave the dog inside to protect her neighbors from his annoying bellowing. It was really very sweet. Ever since I have been letting the dog in and out when my sister goes out of town so that he does not disturb the neighbors.

Summer proved to be a great neighbor to her and an extremely nice person to all of my sister's family. Now that I have a very annoying dog as a neighbor, I think of Summer and her note. She handled the situation very delicately, nicely and managed to maintain a great relationship with her neighbors. I think that is the mark of a really good person.*–Ivy Brock*

When John and Summer first married, all of us descended on them at the house with the pool. There are four siblings: Fran, John, David and Bob, and we all had babies or pre-schoolers. I went into the kitchen to get a Coke from the refrigerator. I accidentally hit the egg holder on the inside of the fridge and dropped an egg. I just cleaned it up and went back to everyone else. The next morning Summer was standing in front of the egg holder counting eggs. She had a dozen—one egg for each of us and a pound of bacon. Finally, after she realized there were only 11 eggs I suggested we scramble them with milk, cut the bacon in small pieces and serve it that way. I never confessed I was the culprit who broke the 12th egg.

Summer was a sweet, naïve young woman but completely overwhelmed by the invasion of Shipps. We loved her then and still now. She'll always be in our hearts. *–Fran Shipp-Nelson*

With Summer at a store survey I asked her where she was going for a break. She informed me she was going to Starbucks or another name brand coffee house to get her latte. Well, when I said to her, "Just get the store brand right here and save yourself a trip," Summer looked like "Shock Theatre." Her response was, "Why, I'd never ever ever use the store brand!" And then she laughed that Summer laugh that only she had and gave me that Summer smile that only she had. *–Neil Barnard*

Summer was always giving me little gifts. Sometimes on the sly she would leave a cute "doggie" bar of soap in my office bathroom, etc. Other times I'd get something special in the mail. She sure did like to surprise people that way. I miss her terribly, especially on our typical projects that she always worked. She was a terrific upbeat gal … so much fun!--*Anita Campbell*

Summer
Unforgettable
Mother of Brandy
Many friends
Extraordinary
Remember always
Summer is the golden thread in the weaving of fabulous family and friends, creating a beautiful tapestry.--*Julie Walters*

We were privileged to have Brandy come to Beaumont, TX on July 16, 2005 to speak at the Kimberly Ann Langwell Candlelight Vigil. Brandy is a lovely lady and we fell in love with her. Brandy has a strong character and her drive and persistence and all her efforts will one day help all missing persons. We believe Brandy has a special purpose on this earth and God will use her to help the plight of the silenced missing. Even in her sadness Brandy has shown that her deep love and affection for her mother didn't have to be overshadowed by sitting still and doing nothing. Brandy chose to take the most negative and painful circumstances and turn it into a positive campaign to find Summer. Brandy is a fighter and will come out victorious for Summer's sake one day soon. We pray that God will give Brandy courage to remain steadfast in her faith and continue her fight to find her Mother. –*Dede and Dale Keene, Founders of AMALP.*

I've been resisting writing something to put in this book and now it's down to the wire. The celebration of Summer is this week. My birthday, Dec. 10, will never be the same. Last year I had a big party at a Crossroads art gallery, and of course Summer was invited. The day before I started getting telephone calls: Have you heard from Summer? Is she coming to your party?" It was all very scary, yet I felt that she would eventually show up. Now a year has gone by and we're having this event. What can I contribute to a book for you? I have many connections to Summer. I've known her a long time, way back from when we were business owners in Westport, and then during the evolution of the Film Society. At one point my son even dated a woman who lived in Summer's house. I would always run into Summer around town—at movies, art galleries, music events, shopping or flea markets, or just out and about.

I was honored to be invited to her garden party/brunch gatherings, which evolved into our Tuesday night ladies supper group, which continued and expanded to include spouses and boyfriends. We all enjoy each other so much. Summer was the catalyst to growing the friendships for the rest of us. Our common link was Summer.

I keep thinking that it took five years for the story of Precious Doe to be fully discovered. It has only been a year since our good friend disappeared. I feel sure that in time we will learn the story of Summer Shipp. With love and fond memories, **Susan Lawrence**

Dear Brandy,

Your mother was a phenomenal friend to all who had the privilege of knowing her. Summer's warm love, gentle kindness and diverse interests were a heavenly gift and treasure to all her friends. Brandy, your mother loved you soooo. Try to reflect her beauty and you will never go wrong. To each of us, friends and family, Summer's love of life, her joy in being alive, her deep compassion for others all are a part of her legacy to each of us.--*Dodie Murphy*

Summer and I met in our Valentine neighborhood because of our dogs. We both had 'em and loved 'em. She'd walk hers past my fenced yard and all the doggies would get excited and bark and fuss. There'd be times I was inside and heard a voice outside. It was Summer having a chat with my dogs.

Over several years we got to be better and better friends, visiting during neighborhood events and going out for fun times. She introduced me to some wonderful people and I was looking forward to us being lifelong pals. And I guess we are, because she has touched me forever with her kind spirit, good humor and beautiful, sparkly self. I will always be grateful for her friendship and I will always miss her. This is all too sad.

—Holly Miller

Summer became sort of my Urban Social Planner, making sure that I didn't miss out on many of the fun, quirky events that our city has to offer. Seems like we didn't let many pass us by. Outings like Girls Night Out with Rainy Day Books or the Valentine's Day chocolate tasting party at the Hyatt or Ballet in the Park. (Even though she tried her best, she never got me to the Elvis parade.) Many events, of course, involved food or coffee or just trying to gather her many special friends to celebrate life.

On our many "cultural" outings, I could always count on Summer for three things:

1. She would invariably show up late

2. She'd likely forget to bring something

3. However, instead, she'd have some special little gift picked up especially for me (like Audrey Hepburn stamps, because she knew I idolized her.)

And best of all, she would always bring her total enthusiasm, joy and that sneaky sense of humor, making any event most wonderful.

Linda Carroll

Summer events: No matter what the activity, with Summer it was always an event. Many weren't well planned but were always a delight... gallery openings, book signings, home tours and art fairs...she was always excited to go. That is, as long as it wasn't too late at night. That makes one event stand out above all others. While in Jamaica, Linda and I had planned to go to a concert. In fact, the trip was timed so we could attend it. I know we talked about it quite a bit before going but I'm not sure that Summer ever fully realized that it started at 9:00 p.m. and lasted through the night until daybreak.

We traveled halfway across the country by mini bus to a little place called Alligator Pond where 40,000 people gathered. Like a trooper, Summer stayed up during the concert through the night. Although dead tired, she was her cheerful self for the return trip home in the morning.

I have great memories of her traveling to Jamaica with us in January. She was the perfect person to take along. Part of my love for Jamaica is the people. In spite of the bad publicity, the majority of Jamaicans are wonderful people, a fact often overlooked by the average American tourist in a hurry. Summer wasn't intimidated at all by the vendors on the beach. Instead of finding them to be obnoxious, she found out their life stories. I don't know how interested she really was in their wares, but whether they made a sale or not, they felt special after talking to Summer. On several occasions she got to spend time with children, where her love really showed.–*Scotti Bickford*

My most recent memory of Summer is running into her at a yoga class over a year ago. She had such a peace and contentedness about her .. . very zen. She just had this glow about her. There's always been such an ease and loveliness that emanated from her. She was always very caring and interested in me whenever our paths crossed. She was just so beautiful— inside and out. She will truly be missed.— *Jane Loutzenhiser*

I fell in love with Summer the minute I met her sporting brightly colored condoms poking off her head. When I think of Summer the word "grace" comes to mind, but also FUN. Summer was the center of fun. I'm blessed to know her. She was never negative about people or life. That is an example I wish to adopt. She was a great listener and a people person. She has been and will be greatly missed.

Brandy, the last year will be the most challenging in your life. You have conducted yourself with amazing dignity and been a tough survivor. Your mom is so proud of you, I am certain. Remember that you have a lot of love behind you. —***Marg Higgins.***

Ahhh Summer! My first knowledge of my dear sister-in-law was through her mom, Cora. "Oh, Summer is going to love having a sister-in-law that has so much sweetness and love; my little girl is the sweetest thing ever. She's always been that way, ever since she was two," said Cora. And over the ten years in the family Summer's name is likened to kindness, joy, health, energy...love. And her love for Brandy and her family always surprised us with more and more generosity and joy. Ahhh, Summer is like the season... bright, warm, faithful and much like the sunflowers she adored, the roses she nurtured and the peonies she claimed as favorite. Her lifetime of "fragrance" will bless us all. —***Carolyn McCullough***

Summer always made me feel like a star. I can see her now—that bright, bright smile and happy dancing eyes. My favorite Summer story is the one she told me about the time she collared Robert Altman at what was then Meiners in Brookside when he was in town to film ***Kansas City***. Summer talked to the great director about his films, praising those she loved. I suppose she thought it

> Sweet Summer, your life has been a blessing to so many of us that were lucky to know you. I wish you were at this party . . . it's exactly what you would have loved. God bless you always. —Tom Finley

only honest to then criticize the movies she felt fell short. Bravo Summer!–
Don Maxwell

Dear Summer: Remember going to Polski Days in KCK? What fun!
Remember the hat party at Marge's? You were a winner. Remember when
I fixed you up with a friend of mine and it turned out you had known him
years ago! We laughed and laughed. We were a lot alike, you and I, with
our animals and our too many friends! Love, **Belinda Borchardt**

Brandy, as one of the endless number of people who lived in your
house, clogging your privacy with your mother, at least you learned to be
open and communal—no small feat. Brandy, your mother thought the sun
rose and set on you. The last time I saw her when I asked about you she
said, "Brandy is amazing." With what you've done this past year I would
certainly agree. Your mother was such a consistently sweet, kind, generous
spirit. And I am so glad I've known you both. **—Georgia Pratt**

My memories of Summer are scattered fragments of brief and daily
interactions I would have with her throughout the year I lived in the
apartment behind her house. Every interaction I ever had with her was
pleasant. Most were inquiries of hers into happenings in my life. She had a
genuine and enthusiastic interest in what I did, projects I was working on
and trips I had made. The best way I could describe the Summer Shipp I
came to know is "beautifully eccentric." She was also charmingly carefree
and often times forgetful. Not neglectful, but more as though she would be
in the middle of something and her attention would be caught and pulled
away by something else. You could follow her trail. I'd sometimes walk up
her driveway or out my front door and find her car doors wide open, or the
side door to her house. She might leave a bag of something by her car and
I'd carry it inside to her kitchen.

She was adorable, truly. What she gave me at the time was a place of
peace and solitude. The apartment building I had lived in previously drew
regular visits from the police and eventually burned down. Summer's
house was a breath of fresh air. After a short time I came to feel truly at
home there. I had the pleasure of witnessing a year of her routine, from
spring cleaning to battening down the hatches for winter. Her smile, voice,

face, and especially the color of her hair, remain impressed into my mind vividly. She is an unforgettable woman and blessed my life with her presence. I'd say I am grateful and pray that no one that knew her ever forgets her.–*Daniel Bartle*

I knew Summer before I actually knew her. As a counselor at The Crittendon Center (for emotionally disturbed young women) in the 70s, there were volunteers of all sorts. One of the favorites was a beautiful lady named Summer Shipp, who would take between three and five young women to her home to swim during the summer. This was a highly coveted privilege, and something that those young women had never before experienced. Only with the best behavior and highest status would a young woman be allowed to go with Summer. What a surprise when I realized that my husband, Rich Hill, and dear friend Lou Jane Temple, both knew Summer. It was after this that we became friends.

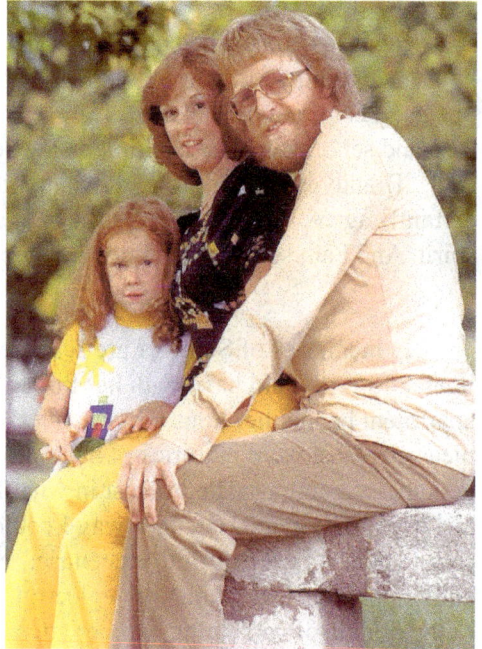

Snapshots:

• She gave many fashion shows for various events and causes. Summer and I were always models—Summer outfitted in form-fitting, cutout rubber dresses; me in Marilyn Monroe type garb.

• When our dear mutual friend, Mary Alys Corcoran, was forced to close her store she had just about run out of friends. Summer was there to the bitter end, helping us close House of Hezekiah with dignity. We left planning a shoe exchange.

Summer was in my life for only a few years, but she touched me as deeply as someone who'd been there for a lifetime. She always had a smile and a compliment for everyone, and when you talked, she seemed to block out everything else around the two of you—she was always interested in what you had to say.

I remember the "Summer" way she said my name when I answered the phone ... how she always had a cup of Starbucks in her hand and managed to find time to stop there, even when she was late for a girls' dinner. I remember how delighted and surprised I was when she (dressed in a boa and a condom hat) ran up to the stage to participate in a costume contest at one of the author readings at Unity Temple. I remember her girlish giggle when she told us about the younger guy who was pursuing her. I loved the way she dressed and the color of her hair. But most of all, I loved her sweetness and her smile, which could make anyone feel like they were her best friend (and she always considered everyone that way!) I have missed her very much this past year . . . and I always will . . . but each time I think about her, I will always smile. —*Lynne Hayes*

I originally met Summer as her interior designer while working at Contemporary Living in the late 1970s. She was married to John and Brandy was just a little girl. What a trio! They were so much fun to be with and so supportive of all my ideas.

It was many years later when I got to know Summer separately from my role as her designer. She came to New York and stayed at my apartment right on Herald Square across from Macy's. It was the early 80s. She was very independent and didn't need me to entertain her at all. In fact, I barely saw her. The most memorable thing that did happen while she was here was she attended the Diana Ross free Central Park concert that was rained out and turned into a riot . ... and she lived to tell about it! She described in quite a lot of detail how everyone was stampeding off in all directions. People were getting trampled on that night. She was an eyewitness to it all. I believe she returned the next night to a lot calmer performance and audience.

Of course, she wanted to get something to bring back for Brandy. Maybe shoes? Summer loved shoes. It was like she couldn't get enough pairs to bring back to KC. I remember her showing me all the pairs that she had bought with quite a lot of pride and enthusiasm before she left. Then she left and I don't believe we ever spoke again. There was no follow up phone call or letter from her. She was here . ... and then she was gone. It was so much like her life. —*Gary Kanter*

Searching for Summer

It is difficult to pinpoint one particular favorite "Summer moment," as I never spent a minute with her that was not a complete joy. As a young woman I was lucky to find a kindred soul in Summer. To this day—and certainly every day in the future—I will remember her smile and ability to find a kindred spirit in everyone she met. The joy Summer found in life's beauties was contagious and a gift to the world. As I mature, I hope to keep her beauty alive by sharing the joy and excitement she gave to others. And speaking of Summer's essence reminds me of the amazing "Shipp glow" that I have seen Brandy radiating in abundance. Summer was so proud and so endearingly sweet when she would tell me all about her incredible daughter, who I have been so lucky to now know as well. She would hold her locket in her hand throughout the day and tell me the cutest stories of Brandy. I could tell how proud she was then and I share that pride in also knowing and loving Brandy—another wonderful woman to always look up to.–*Lizzi*

I met Summer when we were in the same Halloween costume parade at Fric N Frac. She was Little Bo Peep and I was Cleopatra. I came in second to her. Turned out we were Valentine neighbors and Broadway Cafe junkies. We felt like kindred spirits. May those spirits "kindle" on. —*Janet Brown Moss*

This is my typical Summer story—typical of the person she was and why she is so loved.

We had a market research project in Wichita. Driving to Wichita for anything has never been one of my top ten favorite journeys. Our project was three days long. We were staying at a local motel (which did not allow pets) and we drove from KC to Wichita separately. Took me about 3-1/2 hours to get there. Took Summer nearly five hours! She and Alexis took the long route. They stopped along the way to "smell the roses/sunflowers" and avoided the interstate highway system as much as they could.

Summer found beauty everywhere, even on a drive from KC to Wichita. I can't even imagine the beauty she's beholding at this moment and for all eternity.–**Dee Sexton**

There are so many lovely memories it's hard to confine them to a 4 x 5 card. I concentrate on her smile and all the trinkets and silly "fun stuff" we shared, including a Cora's Cake (there was no note, but knew it had to be from Summer because of her mother), a wooden cat from her last trip, many pins "coffee pin" which I'm wearing...a Menopause pin sent with a packet of grape smelling condoms (cracked me up), a Hershey's Kiss pin, to name a few. Then there was the box of chocolates she sent when one of my cats died, a rubber duck, etc. etc.

She visited my mother with me a few times and once we went to Long John Silver's and she fed my mother (she had Alzheimer's Disease). One time when she was with me at my sister's home she said, "Susie, we better go or we'll be late." We both cracked up about that one!

Mainly, I just miss my wonderful friend and always will, but will think of her through smiles and countless happy thoughts. Sleep well, sweet, funny friend, and smile down on us, and especially on Brandy.–**Sue Herrick**

Summer and John and Brandy lived across the street from us on Holmes when Brandy and Tyler were just little girls. Tyler loved to spend the night and Summer always warmly welcomed us. I remember her saying she didn't want any more children because they couldn't possibly be as wonderful as Brandy. I also remember the day she called and said, "My new name is Summer. Please don't call me Dee anymore." **—Mary Stewart**

Who could forget the "Condom Miranda" Halloween outfit? I spent an evening with Summer and some friends at the Imax Theatre at the KC Zoo watching a movie and listening to "The Dolphin Lady." It was one of the best evenings ever.–***Bob Slaughter***

Summer always had very heavy "stuff." Never figured out how she moved stuff around until the Film Festival. Summer had more than enough friends to move her stuff around for her and she was stronger than she looked. She and I moved her giant popcorn machine to the Filmfest and I was more tired than she.–***Jerry Wheeler***

Summer always made you feel like you were of consummate interest to her. When she fixed you in the bright beam of her attention and warmed you with her radiant smile, you felt good. Summer was sunshine.–***Don Maxwell***

Summer and I go back to the 1970s. I sold her cosmetics and went to her and John's theater previews to review all the new movies. I loved Summer. She meant so much to me—such an inspirer or encourager. I loved her pool in her back yard. Brandy and my daughter were born in the same year. —***Alberta Kleitz***

Hi. I'm ***Jessica Landreth,*** 15 years old. I remember one day in July or August I went over to Brandy's. She lived across the street. We were sitting there and I heard the ice cream man. My parents had no money but Summer handed me $5 and said, "Sweetie, get whatever you want." I love you Summer and Brandy.

I loved to go to Summer's for Sunday brunch in the summertime—always a delight, always soooo good! Mimosas and strawberries ... I miss Summer calling me and asking, "Hey, do you want to do something weird?" We always had the best of times.

Summer was an inspiration to me. We both used to joke about our pre-menopausal memory challenges. One night we went to First Fridays. After wandering for a while through one of the galleries we were ready to go. Unfortunately, neither of us could remember where we'd parked and so we wandered another 45 minutes until we found the car.

In all the 20 years I knew her she never uttered a cross or mean word that I can recall. I remember the Bijou, Rocky Horror (I still have a matchbook), Sunday brunch in the back yard at Summer's, and of course, the Elvis parade. She is gone but never forgotten.— ***Kris Wade***

There are so many things about Summer that I will remember, but what strikes me right now is that when I walk through my house I am always finding gifts that she gave me, always for no reason in particular. She was that kind of person; so incredibly thoughtful and made everyone feel that they were important. —***Kathy Connors***

Note left by friend Jim Overman at a Summer Shipp Memorial tribute site:

Every person must struggle against the chaos of nihilism and despair. I knew Summer almost as well as anyone and I can attest that she also dealt with this same struggle. But more than anyone I've ever met, she stood up for truth, for beauty and for the good. Because that's the kind of person she was. It is those qualities in her, contrasted with what happened to her, that has created such an outpouring of emotion. But she would tell us that there is good in everyone. It is the best in human beings, the highest qualities of humanity, that Summer represented. And everyone who knew her recognized that on some level. It is these qualities which can never die.

Thank you, Summer!

Chapter 12: From the Global to the Menial and Back Again

It is late one winter evening when Darrell Wilson hears the doorbell ring at his home at 1819 Redwood Drive. He isn't too concerned about the potential for danger at this house located on the outskirts of Independence. The split level home with several outbuildings has been a great place for Wilson and his family; almost a hideout, in fact. Living at the end of a street with an expansive field next to it is perfect . . . almost like living in the country. It suits his lifestyle, which has included several brushes with the law and even some incarcerations. Still, he is naturally cautious when he goes to the door.

The man standing on his doorstep is no stranger. Darrell has known Jeffery Sauerbry since he was a boy growing up with his nephew, who is the same age. In fact, Darrell feels a little sorry for the kid. He knows he has a violent streak, but sympathizes with him, since he grew up without a father. Wilson opens the door to let Sauerbry in, raising his eyebrows in an unspoken question at the late hour.

"I need to use your computer," offers Sauerbry, brushing by Wilson and heading to the basement rec. room where the desktop computer is located. "Why?" Wilson wants to know.

"Women," Jeffery says cryptically. He has been on Wilson's computer before, trolling for women in chat rooms and on dating websites. While Darrell boots up the computer he talks to his younger friend about the condition of his ill mother, who had also watched Sauerbry grow up. She isn't long for the world and Darrell worries about her looming death. Sauerbry quickly expresses his sympathy. Darrell and friends like Jeffrey are all a pretty tight family group, even though unrelated, and usually come to each other when they need help getting out of legal or financial tight spots.

Darrell watches for a few minutes as Jeffery signs into a chat room, scrolls through the posts and scans the thumbnails of chat participants currently online. He soon excuses himself and goes upstairs for a Diet Coke. When Darrell comes back downstairs ten minutes later, the chat room screen has been replaced by images of the latest news reports on Summer Shipp, the woman who had disappeared last December from Independence. Come to think of it, she had last been seen on Jeffery's street.

"Why are you looking at things on that lady?" Wilson queries Sauerbry. "You can't date a woman who disappeared. Hell, she's probably dead, she's been gone that long."

His young friend turns around in the chair and says, "Well, I got a little story to tell you."

* * * * *

When Brandy Shipp pushes through the familiar doors in the reception area of the International Brotherhood of Iron Workers Monday morning she had already used up her six months of Family and Medical Leave allowance. She really isn't ready to go back to work. All she wants to do is continue to advocate for missing persons and find her mom. But she has a "semi-new" boss; her former supervisor had died from a stroke in March of 2003. She had called Larry, her new boss, that first Friday night when they discovered Summer was missing. He hadn't seemed to grasp what Brandy was going through or understand why she hadn't returned to her job before now.

After Brandy greets all her co-workers and accepts their reassuring hugs and welcomes, Larry calls her into his office.

"Look, I know your mother's missing," Larry says bluntly. "My wife has an eye infection."

Brandy bristles immediately at his tone and the minimizing of her situation.

"This is a place to conduct business," the man continues. "We've all got problems. But we've got work to do here that hasn't been getting done since you've been gone. I suggest you get to it." He dismisses her with a wave of his hand.

As she leaves Larry's office, Brandy starts cursing under her breath in the expert manner that her ironworker colleagues had taught her so well when she first took on her office duties at the training center. She sits at the desk that had once been so familiar and so right, and suddenly it doesn't fit anymore. What is she doing here? This place feels like a foreign country and she is the undocumented worker.

Brandy's real job for the past few months has been to search for her mother. She has appeared on the Nancy Grace show, on the Motel Williams show and countless local and national news stations. She has helped organize fundraisers and vigils for missing persons. She has spoken at the CUE Center for Missing Persons annual conference and arranged for the placement of billboards, bus signs and taxicab placards featuring her mother's photo and the plea for help in locating her. Then there was the memorial tribute event to organize, press conferences and so many special events, plus all the weekly conferences with police for updates.

She has talked to the world about the epidemic of missing persons and about her specific missing loved one. So now she has to go back to this high-pressure, intense job with a boss who doesn't understand?! No way.

Brandy Shipp's letter of resignation is on Larry's desk before the end of the day. She has enough money in savings to survive financially for quite awhile without working. Her reserve funds, really healthy before Summer had disappeared, will still last awhile. And she is sure her neighbors in Gracemore, who have been taking care of her house while she spent all her time at her mom's, are getting tired of that responsibility. It is time to move back home—and to continue her more important job.

So what if she no longer has a paying, full time job? She has other things to do. She can keep calling feature writers and reporters, keep the news alive, like she's done so well these past few months.

Brandy leaves her set of office keys on her desk and packs a few personal items in a box she's retrieved from the store room. Then she glances at the credenza in the reception area and experiences a flashback to one of the last times she had seen that piece of furniture. It was so typical of her mother to leave the bouquet of flowers there to embarrass her. Embarrass her because the flowers were sprinkled with random, partially inflated and colorful condoms that Summer picked up by the dozens at a local Planned Parenthood clinic. Everyone joked about her mother's signature touch and about the "Condom Miranda" hat and trash bag dress Summer often wore to parties.

But her embarrassing gestures didn't end with the condoms. On days Summer and Brandy ate out together, her mother would always tell the waiters that it was her daughter's birthday so a free dessert would appear at the table. Usually it was chocolate, which Brandy hated, but which her mother devoured with relish. Once on Brandy's birthday they were dining at a posh place on the Plaza. Summer had pulled out a gift for Brandy. It was a doll that talked and it was named Summer. Brandy had wanted to melt under the table when her mother had made the doll talk and people seated nearby had looked at the two women curiously, some with raised eyebrows.

Choking back tears, Brandy walks out the doors of the union offices she had entered a few hours ago, wishing she could be embarrassed by her mother just one more time.

*　*　*　*　*

Malisa is trying as hard as possible to keep it together but is now looking over her shoulder every time she is out alone, every time she leaves Nick's to go home at night after work. But it takes a lady with a parrot to prompt her to make a life-changing decision.

The lady's name is Barb and she plays pool with a parrot named Cricket on her shoulder. Malisa finds it amusing and fascinating, especially because the parrot is witty, if foul-mouthed. To pass time when she isn't busy behind the bar, Malisa has even played a few games of pool with Barb and Cricket. Barb gives her a business card one night and later brings in a man she introduces as her husband. They started to befriend this little blonde bartender and disarm her with their friendly and open manners. Barb even suggests they get together sometime outside of Nick's, maybe have dinner together.

But Malisa's contacts through the Friends of Summer website have brought Katie and Kris into her life. These two women, longtime friends of Summer's, are doing everything they can to find clues about her disappearance in order to help the overworked Independence Police Department with their investigation. Of course Kris has the law enforcement background that gives her a lot of credibility and her friend Katie had some really good political connections in Kansas City that prove useful. The two women have interviewed Malisa at length and drop in occasionally at Nick's to give her updates.

When Malisa tells them about the funny, pool-playing couple and their parrot, the two female sleuths go to work with the business card they had given to the bartender. They soon discover Barb's husband works at a cemetery where Jeffrey Sauerbry had worked for a time. The backhoe found in Jeffrey's back yard after Summer's disappearance belongs to the cemetery. Actually, the couple and their parrot know the man with the empty eyes quite well. They have apparently been investigating Malisa at the same time as Kris and Katie have been investigating them. Who knows what would have happened if Malisa had accepted their invitation to go out socially outside of Nick's. Would she have become another missing person?

That's when Malisa makes the decision to quit her job at Nick's. That's when she begins fearing going out in public. That's when she dyes her hair.

Chapter 13: The Squeaky Wheel Tour and The Road to Remember

World-Wide Tour
October 17-November 4, 2006
Hundreds of Artists Banding Together in Events Across the U.S. and in Eight Countries to Reach Over 150 Missing People and Bring ONE Home....

The Grand Emporium Oct. 27, 2006
LIVE! Patrick Lentz, Steve Ewing (from The Urge), Anchondo

3832 Main St.
Kansas City, MO 64111
PLEASE COME OUT AND SUPPORT!!!

Featured Local: Gina Clark (21 years old at the time of her disappearance) was last seen at 8:30 p.m. December 1, 1991, at her Kansas City residence near Mersington and Cleveland. Later that night she called a family member, but the call was disconnected. If you have any info on this case call Kansas City PD at 816-234-5136

Featured Local: Summer Shipp disappeared on Dec. 8, 2004, while conducting door-to-door market research surveys. She was last seen in the 1500 block of W College Terrace in Independence, Missouri. If you have any info on this case, email Brandy Shipp at **friendsofsummer@ gmail.com**

Featured Local: April Wiss was staying with a friend. One night after the friend went to bed, April took her wallet, pager and apartment keys and disappeared. She has not been seen since that time. Date of Birth - 9/1/83 Date Missing - 1/11/00 Missing from - Wichita, Kansas. Wichita Police Dept.

Squeaky Wheel News Release

LOS ANGELES, CA (September 22, 2006) –– GINA for Missing Persons, the internationally acclaimed concert series to raise awareness for those who go missing every year, announces The Squeaky Wheel Tour, October 17-November 4, 2006. This world-wide tour will feature several hundred artists performing in 150 events throughout 50 states and eight countries. The focus of the events is to gain attention for over 150 missing people in the effort to bring at least ONE home.

The international "Squeaky Wheel Tour" honors Gina Bos, who disappeared from Lincoln, Nebraska six years ago. The 19-day tour is the creation of her sister, Jannel Rap, who developed the GINA Concert Series in 2001 bringing together recording artists from all over the U.S. to obtain attention for ALL people who are missing. Every missing child, every missing adult is an important missing person. When loved ones disappear, their family members' lives are devastated. A large part of their lives have been carved out, snatched away, and their only focus is to have their missing loved ones returned.

"Each missing person's story is unique, important and as valuable as the next," said Rap. "If someone took your child or your sister or brother, what would you do? Would you pull down the moon? Would you look under the rock? Would you scream as loud as you could?"

"Would you become the Squeaky Wheel?" added Rap.

"The Squeaky Wheel Tour" will have its kick-off event in Lincoln, Nebraska on October 16-17, 2006 and officially conclude with an event in Little Rock, Arkansas on November 4. In addition, pre- and post-"Squeaky" events will take place starting September 6 with a Webcast concert featuring GINA/LA Women in Music 2006 Contest Winners in Hollywood, CA. A list of the musical artists, locations, and dates are outlined on the following page. This list is also posted at www.411Gina.org and is updated daily.

ABOUT GINA: Singer/songwriter Jannel Rap's sister, Gina Bos, disappeared on October 17, 2000. Gina's story had no scandal, no suspects and lacked the hook and intrigue to get the attention of the national public. Gina had simply vanished after performing at a pub in Lincoln, NE. Six months of slamming doors inspired Jannel into action...and the concept of using entertainment to get attention for the missing was born.

In 2001, Jannel organized a concert series in honor of her sister, called The GINA Sessions, sponsored by GINA for Missing Persons. The series brings together recording artists from all over the country in an effort to raise awareness of all the mothers, fathers, brothers, sisters and children who go missing every year. In addition, through GINA (www.411Gina.org) Jannel has produced a television series called America Lost and FOUND, and now hosts a monthly international webcast featuring missing persons from around the globe.

MISSING PERSONS FROM MISSOURI
www.friendsofsummer.com

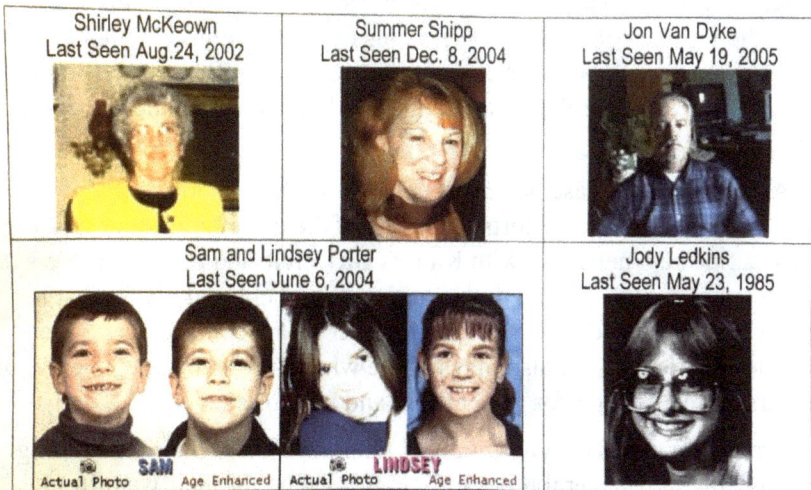

A poster from the CUE Center's Road to Remember Tour

* * * * * *

First it was Precious Doe, a small girl whose decapitated body was found in a Kansas City park in 2001. A few days later her head was found nearby in a black trash bag.

Then, of course, there were the Porter children, Sam and Lindsey, who had disappeared in 2004 from the Sugar Creek area of Kansas City after their dad picked them up for a scheduled visitation. The dad remained tight-lipped even as he sat in a prison cell, refusing to tell investigators anything and seemingly relishing his ability to punish his ex-wife. Dan Porter finally confessed that he shot Sam, 7, and Lindsey, 8, and buried them in the woods.

Then came the mysterious disappearance of Summer Shipp in late 2004, followed in 2007 by Kara Kopetsky, who went missing after she walked out of Belton High School. Later, Jessica Runions disappeared, also from Belton High School, and both girls were connected to a man named Kylr Yust. Their remains were eventually found near each other in the same wooded area.

Kansas City has had what seems like a proportionately high number of high-profile missing persons cases for a city of its size. The community has responded with collective anguish, but also with positive action, such as memorial walks, candlelight vigils and street corner activism. In some cases, the families of the missing persons network with each other and share tips on how to keep the cases in the public eye. Brandy and John Shipp visited Kara Kopetsky's parents, and later Brandy called on Jessica Runion's family.

As her mother's case begins to fade from news reports, Brandy intensifies her advocacy efforts on behalf of the other families of missing persons. She also networks with Kansas City civic and political leaders and gets to know the key people in the city's arts and cultural circles that her mother had circulated in so freely before her disappearance. Her father's influence and leadership also plays a role when they are offered the use of the Screenland Theater for fund raisers and memorial events.

Brandy becomes heavily involved with the CUE Center for Missing Persons, traveling several times to North Carolina for their waterfront vigils, for training workshops and annual conferences. She travels to Beaumont, Texas to speak at a vigil in honor of Kimberly Langwell and for America's Missing, Lost and Abducted (AMALP) Foundation Ministry. The case is eerily reminiscent of Summer Shipp's. Kimberly is last seen in front of a drug store in Beaumont, TX. Her vehicle is located at a shopping center near her home, locked with personal belongings inside, including her cell phone.

Brandy Shipp's networking skills and determination may have rubbed off on others as she pleads the case of missing persons. In February of 2007 she works with Kelly Jolkowski of Project Jason for new model legislation aimed at establishing procedures for the handling of missing persons and identified remains, including the use of DNA analysis. The Summer Shipp Act is introduced in the Missouri Legislature by Rep. Bryan Pratt as HB 757 but did not make it out of committee.

Brandy's efforts touch Alonzo Washington, a well-known Kansas City activist, who organizes an event called "Corner of Hope." On four weekends in February of 2006 he gathers family members connected to unsolved area homicides and missing persons like Summer Shipp. They hand out flyers to raise community awareness and plead for clues to help solve the mysteries.

In December of 2006, on the anniversary week of Summer's disappearance, the Friends of Summer team up with the Achieve Foundation to stage a workshop at the Screenland Theater to teach women some self-protection measures. This event follows the Squeaky Wheel Tour at the Grand Emporium that features Summer's story, as well as other local missing persons.

Then in June of 2007, Brandy's favorite organization, the CUE Center, holds its Fourth Annual Road to Remember Tour with a rally stop at 47th and Main in Kansas City. The tour highlights all the missing persons cases in Kansas City, including Shirley McKown, Sam and Lindsey Porter, Jody Ledkins, Jon Van Dyke, Summer Shipp and Kara Kopetsky. It brings a huge turnout and lots of media attention.

Just a few short months after the tour what is left of Summer Shipp's body and some of her clothing is found by fishermen in the Little Blue River.

Chapter 14: Dropping Out of the Club

October 2007

Janice Cogburn was Brandy Shipp's Electric Shock Sister. That's what the guys at the Builder's Association nicknamed the duo the day that Janice arrived at work with a curly perm. Normally her blonde hair was straight as a board, so it got some attention when she showed up for her secretary's job at the Painter's Union. Brandy was her counterpart at the Ironworkers office and had always had "big hair." The shock sister nickname immediately stuck to Janice and helped to cement the friendship the two women already enjoyed.

When Brandy later left Kansas City for Europe, Janice always made a point of keeping in regular contact by phone, Skype or email. So when Janice first heard the news about fishermen finding a body in the Little Blue River, she knew in her heart that it was Summer's body in that muddy river bank. Something compelled her to immediately jump in her truck and drive to the scene where workers were already busy excavating.

When Janice returned home, she logged onto her Skype account and connected with Brandy, even though she knew it was probably about 3 a.m. in Poland. When the connection went through, Brandy and Jeff had been without Internet for two days. They had just pulled up stakes in Zandavoort, The Netherlands, and landed in Warsaw, where Jeff had an exciting new job opportunity. But "excited" would not be a good description of Brandy's mood when they landed in this gray, depressing city.

In fact, she found that the rested calm she had experienced after several months of riding a bike up and down the North Sea beach in The Netherlands, with her Australian Shepard, Chassy, trotting along beside her, was quickly evaporating.

When she had flown to Western Europe at Jeff's invitation several months before she had been numb, still running on auto-pilot. She had jumped at the chance to escape the stasis of Summer's missing persons case. By the time of her departure to join Jeff, the once weekly meetings with police had lengthened to every other week, then only to once a month. There was no progress, no new information or clues as to Summer Shipp's whereabouts. The psychics had even stopped calling or leaving messages on the website.

Brandy was so ready for a break... something different...anything... when Jeff Chace had suggested she join him in The Netherlands. He had already been one of her anchors and best supports in the ongoing search and publicity efforts, helping by traveling with her to several CUE conferences and special events in Kansas City.

Thanks to Aunt Fran's job with an airline, Brandy could fly at a discount pretty much as often as she wanted. That would prove useful in the next week, as she was about to discover.

"Hey Brandy! How are you doing, honey," asks her concerned friend Janice back in Kansas City.

"Oh, I'm just fine, but we've been without internet until just now," says Brandy. "And we just got a washer and dryer. Can you imagine? If you have even a washer in Poland, you're rich," laughs Brandy.

"Oh, dear,...um...I'm going to have to go. I'll talk to you later! Bye!" Janice abruptly ends the Skype call, leaving Brandy totally puzzled as to why her friend, who normally keeps her on the phone or skype for hours, would hang up so suddenly.

In a few short hours Brandy will learn the news that Janice had not felt she should announce. She learns through separate calls from her dad and Nomi and Independence detectives that her mother's body has been located by fishermen on the banks of the Little Blue River, only about seven miles from where she was last seen. Brandy calls Janice back to let her know she understands the reason for the abrupt ending of the earlier conversation.

"It just wasn't my place to tell you," Janice explains. "It was your dad's place."

Then Janice goes into high-gear friend mode, setting up a memorial tent at the excavation site. Under that tent friends of Brandy and Summer will gather to sign a large poster and leave memorial mementos as they try to stay on top of excavation efforts nearby.

So, instead of helping Jeff get established in Poland, Brandy hops on a Delta flight and heads home.She is running out of money anyway, having dipped into her substantial savings to finance the publicity and search efforts.

When she arrives in Kansas City, Brandy meets with police and county prosecutors to go over the gruesome details of the fishermen's discovery. Numbly, she then helps organize the details for a Celebration of Life service for her mother, once again to be held at the Screenland Theater, thanks to the generosity of Butch and Marti Rigby. Speakers include Alvin Brooks, Police Chief Fred Mills, Rev. Sam Mann and Jan Marcason. Well-known locals David Basse and Ida McBeth provide the heartfelt music.

The little that was found of Summer Shipp's body is later buried in a child's casket in a private graveside service at the Iberia Cemetery in Southeast Missouri. She had been missing for almost three years.

* * * * *

Brandy's voice trembles slightly as she addresses the people gathered for the April 2008 CUE roundtable in Wilmington, North Carolina.

In a tribute to her mother, she begins hesitantly. "She was just doing her job, going from house to house, knocking on doors. That was the last day she was ever seen. Since that day my life will never be the same."

She continues, gaining strength from the supportive looks she is getting from people in the audience who know all too well what she has gone through.

"I never realized that someone's life could change so drastically, so permanently in one day, with no notice whatsoever. I became a member of a club which I never intended on joining. That club consists of people who have had a loved one who has gone missing."

"I believe that God has given me the inner strength to face reality. I chose to be proactive instead of crawling into my shell. I chose to focus all day, every day on the search for my mother. With the help of friends, family, the community, media and so many wonderful groups like the CUE Center, I was able to get my mother's story out there in the public eye any and every way I could. And, as many of you here heard me say, 'I will never give up.'"

Brandy pauses, trying to keep the tears from flowing so she can finish her prepared remarks. "As the days went by and the weeks and the months, I remained dedicated, even though I knew the odds were against my mother ever coming home. I continued to believe she would."

"In October, when my mother's body was found, people told me that was closure. That was not closure. There will never be closure. This will be part of the rest of my life, no matter what happens."

She continues, a tear rolling down her cheek. "This will be my fourth year of attending the CUE Center's Vigil for Missing Persons. But I never thought I would see my mother's picture among those who were no longer missing. I now realize I will never again hear her cheerful laughter or see her stop and smell the roses as she so often did, literally. I will always remember her telling me how much she loved me, how she adored her dogs like they were her children, how she would always find the good in people, no matter what."

Brandy concludes her remarks with freely flowing tears and a poem, adding, "My mother will be alive in my heart forever, as well as in the hearts of the thousands of people she touched."

If roses grow in heaven Lord, please pick a bunch for me, place them in my mother's arms and tell her they're from me.

Tell her that I love her and miss her, and when she turns to smile, place a kiss upon her cheek and hold her for awhile.

Because remembering her is easy,– I do it every day,

But there's an ache within my heart that will never go away. (Kirsten Preus)

As Brandy finishes reading that poem, she knows immediately that it will somehow mark her mother's grave. She hasn't even left Wilmington when she starts designing the tombstone that will bear those words.

Chapter 15: Trials Continue... Now in Courtrooms

Attorney John Kurtz has a long-standing habit of identifying emotionally with his clients. He often becomes so invested in the folks who seek his help that he goes well beyond what is generally required of an attorney. And it's usually because he admires his clients' courage or their contributions to society.

When well-known community activist Mamie Hughes became his client years before, John was so intent on having this energetic woman record her fascinating personal history that he even provided the assistance of his own para-legal, Patricia Irvin. She took dictation from Mamie on several occasions, and then compiled a manuscript. Kurtz also strongly encouraged another local black leader, Alvin Brooks, to write his autobiography.

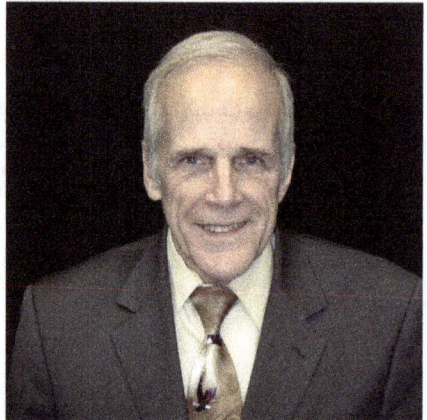

In his 38 years of civil litigation John Kurtz has always been touched by wrongful death cases. When Brandy Shipp comes to the offices of Hubbard & Kurtz on Walnut in downtown Kansas City, shortly after her mother's remains had been laid to rest, John is already familiar with her struggles. Who wouldn't have noticed the billboards and taxicab signs seeking help in locating Summer Shipp? Who hadn't been totally captivated by Summer's stunning redheaded daughter as she issued countless public appeals for help in finding her missing mother?

It takes only a few minutes of meeting with Brandy Shipp for John Kurtz's compassion to take up her cause. She wants to ensure that other door-to-door marketing reps would not be working without safety precautions and training. He emphasizes to Brandy and to John and Naomi

Shipp that the possibilities of winning a wrongful death lawsuit against Roper Worldwide, the company that sent Summer Shipp to Independence that day to do surveys, are remote at best. Still, he thinks it is worth the chance of trying to hold the company responsible. The suit will claim Roper was negligent in sending Summer out to do door-to-door surveys without providing her with equipment necessary to defend herself properly. The suit will also claim Roper should have researched the areas for sexual predators and past criminal activity, provided warnings about the danger involved in the work, and sent surveyors out in groups rather than alone.

The Shipp suit makes it all the way to the Eighth Circuit Court of Appeals after it is kicked out in district court. Brandy, John and Naomi accompany John Kurtz to St. Louis for the appeal before a three-court judge panel. Several weeks later they get the negative decision they feared.

If all he cared about was winning, John Kurtz would never have taken such a long-shot case. Prior to taking on the Shipp suit he had prevailed in another wrongful death case, involving another woman named Brandy. She also was a redhead like Brandy Shipp and was the only daughter of her parents. They persisted in getting justice for her after she was murdered by her husband.

John Kurtz still agonizes about Brandy Shipp not getting relief in her civil case. But he hopes it might have contributed in some way to a change in procedures by marketing companies. Rhetorically, he poses a question about other companies like Avon, Fuller Brush and Kirby Vacuum, all of whom have abandoned door-to-door sales. John wonders, was it purely economics that drove these decisions or were there too many situations in urban areas with increased exposures to potentially dangerous situations?

* * * * *

November, 2011

A black-robed Roger Prokes sits on the dais of one of the courtrooms in the Jackson County Courthouse in Independence. In a self-effacing manner that had already surfaced in the preliminary motions in State of Missouri vs. Jeffery Sauerbry, Prokes references his Northwest Missouri roots, almost apologizing for them as a visiting judge. He seems to tiptoe softly through proceedings in a place where grand juries frequently hand down indictments, as opposed to standard operating procedures in rural courts where Judge Prokes normally presides.

Despite his humble manner, the judge who has been assigned to this controversial case has a decidedly solid legal background, having served as a private attorney for 24 years and as an adjunct professor of education law before being elected to the 4th Circuit Court in November of 2000.

Today, July 30, 2012, Judge Prokes looks down at the prosecuting attorneys and the public defender in this case with the same mild manner that has endeared him to attorneys and witnesses on either side of his cases.

"Okay," he reads, peering over his horn-rimmed glasses. "The next motion I have that has been scanned in here is a motion *in limine* to exclude any evidence that the defendant was a suspect in another matter, or any reference whatsoever to that matter. Does the defense object to that? Excuse me, let me get my mouth working right today. Does the plaintiff object to that, the State?"

Prosecutor Allison Dunning replies, "No. I think this one specifically involves an investigation involving a victim by the name of Summer Shipp, and the State would not object to that."

Leon Munday, a Missouri Public Defender, interjects, " Your Honor, I appreciate that. If I could just kind of elaborate a little bit. And as you may or may not know, the Summer Shipp case is a very high-profile case that has gone on. It's instantly available on the Web and is pretty well-known. And I just have a great fear that should that arise at all – I don't have a fear, I know that I will be asking for a mistrial and I suspect in that event that request would be taken very seriously because of the overwhelming prejudice."

Munday continues, "So I just would like for everyone – and I'm sure the State is not going to intentionally get into it. We have some loose-cannon witnesses that I'm just deathly afraid that they're going to volunteer something. And I would encourage any kind of whatever we can do to keep them on target and not straying into this forbidden territory, I would be grateful for."

Without any hesitation, Judge Prokes responds, "Well , I'm going to sustain the motion *in limine* and the State has heard what you said."

* * * * *

The first time Malisa Jennings met Brandy Shipp face-to-face, Brandy was paying for groceries with her debit card. Malisa recognized the name on the card instantly.

When she looked up from the cash register at the red-haired woman making a purchase at Dirty Don's in Raytown, a bargain store where the former bartender had gone to work in 2006, she recognized her face from the many times Brandy had been on the news.

"You don't know me," she said softly so other customers could not hear, "But I'm the bartender from Nick's in Independence. I served Jeffrey Sauerbry the day your mom disappeared," she said. Then Malisa rushed around the counter to give Brandy a huge hug. The two women clung tightly to each other, both erupting in a cascade of tears. Brandy then remembered that when Malisa had originally contacted her through the Friends of Summer website, she had referred Malisa to John Underhill, the private investigator. She had been so distraught in those early days, so overwhelmed, she couldn't absorb all of the clues to her mother's disappearance, clues like what Malisa had offered then.

The two women didn't have much time to talk that day at Dirty Don's, but that would soon change.

Like Brandy, Malisa was still suffering from the fallout of Summer's disappearance–the PTSD kind of suffering. Jeffery Sauerbry had continued to haunt her days, skulking around corners, leering at her and reminding her that he was watching her. She took those frequent and terrifying encounters as silent warnings for her not to offer any more information or assistance to investigators.

Before starting to work at Dirty Don's, Malisa had changed her hair color. She had stopped bartending. She was trying to rebuild her life but was always looking over her shoulder.

A few days after her surprise encounter with Brandy, Detective Joseph Christianson from the Independence Police Department contacted Malisa. Apparently, they were reopening the case against Sauerbry in regard to Summer's disappearance. He met with Malisa and took her statement again on July 26, 2012, just days before the William Kellett murder trial began.

Malisa had just been mulling over the coincidental meetings with Brandy and the detective on a day when she was by herself as lead cashier at Dirty Don's. The meetings were so close together, almost like they were divinely orchestrated. She would later ask herself if the next event was also a type of morbid serendipity.

She was looking at the front door when Jeffery Sauerbry himself walked into the store. He seemed angry, agitated and came directly to the checkout counter where she was standing and looked intently at her.

"I know you from someplace," he insisted menacingly. When she didn't answer, trying desperately to control the whole-body quivering that immediately began from confronting her biggest nightmare, Sauerbry's agitation only increased. If he recognized the face under her now-brunette hair, he couldn't quite place it. And Dirty Don's was not even close to where he lived. Why was he here?

For fifteen minutes, Sauerbry ranted incoherently about how he was being persecuted and framed before finally giving up. Malisa had just stared at him uncomprehendingly during the diatribe. Thankfully, a customer stepped up to the cash register just as Sauerbry's agitation reached a fever pitch. He then turned and walked out and she realized he had not shopped at all.

Malisa went outside Dirty Don's to make sure he had really left and screamed until she was hoarse. She could not stop shaking, realizing she could have said something that would have tipped him off to her identity.

* * * * *

July, 2012

By the time the State of Missouri vs. Jeffrey S. Sauerbry, Case No. WD 75597, finally began in July of 2012, Judge Roger M. Prokes had already heard and denied a motion by the defense to dismiss the case based on prosecutorial delay. After all, it had been 14 years since July 4, 1998, the date that William Kellett was shot, stabbed and had his head almost severed inside the travel trailer he was living in at E & L Motors, a used car lot on Highway 24 in Independence. In the interim, three of the original witnesses had died.

While Sauerbry had been arrested early on in connection with the trial, and had been in jail from July 1998 through March of 1999, the state had not filed murder charges against him until 2009. When the matter finally came before Judge Jack Grate Jr. in October of 2010 for a competency hearing and again in October of 2011 for pre-trial motions, Prosecutors Tammy Dickinson, Allison Dunning, Megan Wiese and Ted Hunt were forced to withdraw the case. Judge Grate had ruled the testimony of one of the prosecution's key witnesses inadmissible. So the prosecutors immediately re-filed the case, along with a request for change of judge.

In the re-filed case in 2012, Public Defender Munday complained to Judge Prokes that he had been required to prepare for trial twice now. He wasn't getting paid. The Missouri Public Defender's Office was severely understaffed. Still, throughout the upcoming trial, Munday would demonstrate the same tenacity as any highly paid defense attorney in trying to keep Sauerbry from serving life in prison without parole, the sentence required in this first degree murder case. As a concession to the defense, Judge Prokes allowed the admission of testimony given to police by the now deceased three witnesses, recorded during the initial investigation in 1998.

Jury selection began on Monday, July 30, 2012. By the next morning, the trial began with the State calling detectives and medical examiners to the stand to re-create their investigations into Kellett's murder.

Brandy Shipp, her father John and stepmother Naomi sat in the second row during the trial, right behind William Kellett's daughter. They had all been warned strenuously against saying anything inside the courtroom or outside that could be overheard by jurors or spectators. They were to say nothing that would indicate there was any connection between the Summer Shipp case and Jeffrey Sauerbry.

Brandy sat with her victim's advocate and Kellett's daughter with hers. They all watched and listened, sometimes in horror, as crime scene investigators and lab technicians detailed the manner in which the victim had been attacked—first with a bullet of incorrect caliber from a sawed-off shotgun. Testimony revealed that the bullet had entered Kellett's neck and just lodged there harmlessly, since it had barely enough velocity to break the skin. Instead, the death had been caused by multiple stab wounds and a slashed throat, according to the expert witnesses. There were signs on the victim's body of defensive wounds to his arms and hands, indicating he had tried to fend off the attack.

With the testimony of crime scene investigators, the prosecutors took the jury through the discovery of the sawed-off shotgun and a large knife found in the possession of Jeffrey Sauerbry just a few days after the killing. At the time those weapons were put in the evidence lockers at the Independence Police Department, there were no traces of Kellett's blood on the knife. Years later forensic specialists, during pre-trial investigations, had taken the knife apart and found positive traces of blood. In the autopsy files they had also found a notation about finding traces of "flash" burns from un-ignited gunpowder on Kellett's neck and torso in a pattern consistent with the direction the gun was fired from outside the trailer and through the window screen. The bullet recovered from the victim's neck was ruled likely to have been shot through the sawed-off shotgun that had been in Sauerbry's possession.

The ballistics and science of the investigation would soon combine with the damaging testimony of an alleged confession by Sauerbry to a family friend to help seal his fate.

* * * * *

When Diana Reno Huffman took the stand on Wednesday, August 1, she did so out of sight of the jury. The fact that she was in a wheelchair and using oxygen could have given the jurors some sympathy for her that might have weighed too heavily into their consideration of the case. Or so Defense Attorney Munday argued before Judge Prokes. Huffman was already seated in the witness stand when the jury was led in.

After Huffman identified Jeffrey Sauerbry seated between his two defense attorneys, Prosecutor Allison Dunning approached Huffman, maintaining a respectful distance from the stand, and began to question her key witness.

Prosecutor Dunning: How is it that you know Jeffrey Sauerbry?

Huffman: I've known him since he's been about 12 years old. He grew up in the old neighborhood where I was raising my son

Dunning: And who is your son?

Huffman: Barry Holcomb.

Dunning:. Did your son know Jeffrey Sauerbry?

Huffman: Yes. They were best friends.

Dunning: How long were they best friends?

Huffman: From 12 years old till now.

Dunning: Okay. They're still friends? They still communicate?

Huffman: I think they still write.

Dunning: And when – From the time he was 12 until sometime in the future would Jeffrey Sauerbry come to your home?

Huffman: Yes.

Dunning: All right. Did you consider him a friend yourself?

Huffman: Yes.

Dunning: All right. And did there come a period of time where he would sometimes actually stay with you in your home?

Huffman: He lived at my home for a couple months, I think.

Dunning: Okay.

Huffman: About two months.

Dunning: All right. Now, I want to talk about that two-month time frame. Did you in July of 1998, I think it was July 7th of 1998, do you remember having a Detective Bob West come by your home to ask about the whereabouts of Jeffrey Sauerbry?

Huffman: Yes, I do.

Dunning: Now, back just prior to that period in 1998, is that when Mr. Sauerbry lived with you in your home?

Huffman: Yes.

Dunning: Now, at that time in 1998 – and he stayed with you. Where did he stay in your house?

Huffman: He stayed upstairs in one of the bedrooms. I think it was the front bedroom.

Dunning: Okay. Was it near your bedroom?

Huffman: Yes.

Dunning: And how did he come and go from the house?

Huffman: By bicycle.

Dunning: Okay. Did he ride his bicycle often?

Huffman: He rode it to work and back, and everywhere he was going to go unless someone else took him.

Dunning: Okay. He was known to ride a bike as his main transportation?

Huffman: At that time.

(Testimony that followed included information about Huffman finding a gun and learning Sauerbry had sawed it off in her garage. She told police about it when they came to her home looking for him. She then went to the station to identify it.)

Dunning: Okay. Did you ever know the defendant to carry a knife?

Huffman: In his boot.

Dunning: Do you remember what kind of knife it was?

Huffman: No.

Dunning: Okay. Now, before Mr. Kellett was murdered, did you ever talk to the defendant about Mr. Kellett?

Huffman: Yes. He came home sometimes from the car lot. He was working up there part time, if I remember. He was real upset about him. He said he was always messing with him.

Dunning: Did he say what he was doing to mess with him?

Huffman: Just messing with him, picking at him.

Dunning: Okay. And did he ever give you any examples of stuff that he would do?

Huffman: Yeah, it seems like it but I can't really remember now what it was. Because he was very upset about it. I told him he needed to quit there. If it bothered him that bad, go get a job somewhere else.

Dunning: And to your knowledge did he go get another job somewhere else?

Huffman: No, he kept going there. He had another job, though, at the restaurant.

Dunning: Okay. But he kept going back to the lot as well?

Huffman: Yes.

Dunning: All right. And do you remember if you spoke to him about that subject once or more than once?

Huffman: We spoke about two times.

Dunning: Okay. And where was it that you talked to him?

Huffman: At my home, in the back yard once.

Dunning: Okay. Do you know about how close in time...I guess at some point did you find out that Mr. Kellett had died?

Huffman: Yeah, it was just like about a week–maybe two weeks later.

Dunning: Okay. But one or two weeks between those two things?

Huffman: Yes.

Munday: I'm going to object. She said two then she comes in with a question that says one.

Dunning: I thought she said one–a week or two.

Judge Prokes: I'll sustain that objection.

Dunning: Can you give me a time frame between the last time you could have talked about Mr. Kellett and the time that Mr. Kellett was killed?

Huffman: Maybe two weeks.

Dunning: Okay. What was Jeffrey Sauerbry's demeanor? What was his emotion when he talked about Mr. Kellett?

Huffman: He was really upset. Would sweat. Jeff didn't act right. He just didn't act right. He hadn't for the whole time he'd been at my house. He acted different. This really seemed to bother him really bad.

Dunning: All right. Now, after learning that Mr. Kellett had died, did you have a conversation with the defendant about that?

Huffman: Yes.

Dunning: And can you tell us where that was?

Huffman: It seems like it was in my kitchen.

Dunning: Okay. And would you agree, therefore, that that was sometime after Mr. Kellett died?

Munday: I'm going to object to the leading, Your Honor.

Judge Prokes: Sustained.

Dunning: Was Mr. Kellett already dead when you had this conversation?

Huffman: Yes.

Dunning: And was Mr. Sauerbry not in jail when you had this conversation?

Huffman: Yes.

Dunning: All right. Now, what is it that you talked to him about?

Huffman: Mr. Kellett dying.

Dunning: And what did he say?

Huffman: He said he killed him.

Dunning: Could you tell us how that came up?

Huffman: Yeah. The police had . . . he said they wasn't going to F with him anymore.

Dunning: Okay. And did he actually say F or did he . . .

Huffman: No, he used the word.

Dunning: Okay. And did he give you any details about how that had taken place?

Huffman: Yes. He had told me that...it seems like they'd been playing poker a little earlier. And he was F-ing with him and that he went back . . . he left and went back and made noise on the side of the trailer. And when he stuck his head up in the window, he shot him in the face...or he shot him.

Dunning: Did he say anything about hurting him in any other way?

Huffman: I don't remember him saying any other thing. He said they got into it.

Dunning: Okay. Did you ask him anything about any evidence?

Huffman: No–yeah, he did. He said that somebody he rode with, that he had a backpack and he put it in the trash at McDonald's.

Dunning: And why did that come up?

Huffman: Because I didn't want the gun in my house.

Dunning: Okay. And did he make any comments about throwing those items away?

Huffman: Yeah. He said he threw them in the dumpster at McDonald's.

Dunning: Okay. And did he comment on anything further about that?

Huffman: No.

* * * * *

Dunning: Now, did you ultimately learn that he had been arrested?

Huffman: Yes, later.

Dunning: Okay. And when the police spoke to you, do you believe that you told them all the information you had when they spoke to you?

Huffman: No, I didn't.

Dunning: Why not?

Huffman: I was afraid.

Dunning: And why were you afraid?

Huffman: Jeff wasn't hisself anymore. I was afraid of him.

Dunning: And had he done anything specifically that caused you to feel that way?

Huffman: Because after telling me . . . my little girl, we slept together. She woke me up and he was standing in the hallway of my home in the dark and I could see him standing there. He stood there for a long time. It scared me.

Dunning: And what time of day was this?

Huffman: It was at my bedtime. It was late. I don't know what hour of the morning. Because my little girl was woke up and seen him there first. And he was standing in the hall, and I don't know if he was just standing there looking at us. I don't know. I felt not safe.

Dunning: Did you talk to him about that incident?

Huffman: No.

Later that day the defense questioned the witness.

Munday: But it's your sworn testimony here today that on July 7th, when you had your first contact with Detective West, Mr. Sauerbry had already confessed to you but you decided to withhold that information from the police?

Huffman: Yes, I did.

Munday: And you withheld that information because you were scared?

Huffman: Yes, I was scared of him.

Munday: But you provided all this other information to the police to help them find him, know where he was, and so forth. Or you may have, you can't recall?

Huffman: That's correct.

Munday: Okay. So if you said you hadn't seen Mr. Sauerbry since July the 1st, would that have been a lie?

Huffman: It was a lie.

Munday: Okay.

Huffman: I tried to uninvolve myself.

Munday: Okay. And so lying to the authorities who are investigating a murder is something that you feel pretty comfortable with, I take it?

Dunning: Your Honor, I'm going to object to the argumentative nature of the question.

Judge Prokes: Overruled. It's cross examination.

Munday: Lying to the authorities about a murder is something that you feel comfortable doing?

Huffman: No, I didn't feel comfortable doing it.

Munday: But you did it?

Huffman: Yes, I did.

Munday: So whether you feel comfortable doing it or not, you're perfectly capable of doing it?

Huffman: I perfectly was in a bad spot. I've known this child since he's been 12 years old. It's really hard to do that to somebody that you've known since a child. At the same time I was afraid of him. And I'm sorry I lied to them. I did what I had to do. But . . .

Munday: Were you afraid that he could do something from the jail to hurt you?

Huffman: Do you know how many times he's gotten out of jail?

Munday: Your Honor, could we approach?

(Counsel approached the bench and the following conversation took place:)

Munday: I'm going to move to strike, and, you know, she's now answering questions that aren't responsive and it scares the devil out of me.

Dunning: I think that question invited a response that he could not have accounted for. I don't mind if you move to strike it, but he needs to be careful with her because she has a lot of information.

Judge Prokes: I'm going to strike the question. I don't think necessarily we expected it, so I'm going to order it be stricken, the thing about his being in jail. I'll order the jury to disregard the comment about the number of times Jeffrey Sauerbry has gotten out of jail.

The proceedings then returned to open court.

Judge Prokes: The jury is instructed to disregard the witness's comment about the number of times that Jeffrey Sauerbry has gotten out of jail.

Munday: So he's in jail and you have this information that you say he confessed to you that he committed that murder, but you're afraid to tell the police that. Is that your testimony here today?

Huffman: Not only afraid, I hated to do it.

Munday: Okay. Do you recall asking Detective West, is Mr. Sauerbry still in custody?

Huffman: I may have.

Munday: Well, but you don't know?

Huffman: I can't remember.

Munday: Okay. And did you tell Detective West, I'm afraid of Jeffrey Sauerbry?

Huffman: I may have.

Munday: Did you tell Detective West that Mr. Sauerbry had paranoid thoughts about the DEA implanting a camera in his eyeball or something like that?

Huffman: Yes.

Munday: And that he was a threat to his mother, calling and telling Detective West that?

Huffman: I think so. I think Jeffrey called me from jail when they had him and thought I was trying to set him up and that–switch places with him and my son. And it made me more afraid of him.

Munday: Uh-huh. So you told the detectives a lot of information about Jeffrey Sauerbry, didn't you?

Huffman: Yes, I probably did.

Munday: Now, you didn't have any...so 11 years goes by; is that right?

Huffman: Yes.

Munday: And you never say anything?

Huffman: Never, no.

Munday: And not until Detective Christiansen makes contact.

Huffman: Right.

Later in re-cross examination ...

Munday: So you're here today to do the right thing?

Huffman: Yes.

Munday: But for 11 years you didn't do the right thing?

Huffman: No, I didn't.

Munday: Thank you, ma'am.

That day's trial concluded with testimony by an Independence detective who notified William Kellett's next-of-kin on the day his body was found. On Thursday, Aug. 2, 2012, Detective Joseph Christiansen took the stand again to go over his activities upon reopening of the investigation. Prosecution and defense asked him about reviewing forensic information on the gun and knife found in Sauerbry's possession and about his dealings with the reluctant witness, Diana Reno Huffman.

The State called three more witnesses, including Detective Jeff Lawhon (who had interviewed Earl Tharp, owner of the car lot on the day the investigation opened in 1998), Mary Dudley, M.D., the county's chief medical examiner, and Katherine May, a ballistics expert at the police crime lab. After reviewing the evidence and photos of the autopsy performed by a predecessor, Dr. Dudley determined that the cause of William Kellett's death was due to multiple sharp force injuries and the manner of death was by homicide.

At the end of the day on Thursday, Leon Munday called only one witness for the defense, Detective Robert West, before resting. When the court reconvened at 9 a.m. on Friday, Aug. 3, the attorneys presented closing arguments and Judge Prokes gave the defendant an opportunity to testify on his own behalf. Jeffrey Sauerbry did not take advantage of that chance.

The jury left to deliberate at 11:48 a.m., requesting access to all the case evidence at 1:08 p.m. At 3:16 p.m. the jury foreperson, Angela Cottrell, handed the judge the verdict envelope: Jeffrey Sauerbry was found guilty of murder in the first degree.

Before he left the courthouse, the newly convicted Independence man was served with another grand jury indictment charging him with the first degree murder of Summer Shipp.

Chapter 16 - Jeffrey Sauerbry's Murder Indictment and Trial

August 3, 2012

"Brandy, where are you?" her friend Connie asks breathlessly. "You need to get back here right now. The victim's advocate just called me saying they're trying to find you!"

Brandy and Connie and a score of friends and supporters have just sat through the William Kellett murder trial and a surprisingly quick guilty verdict. That courtroom had been extra crowded as the jury filed back in. All the police officers who had testified were back, swelling the spectators to more than 50 anxious souls. Those close to the case had been surprised it had taken the jury just a little over three hours to reach their unanimous decision.

Brandy and her family members are anxious to get out of that stuffy courtroom and end the agony of sitting through days of testimony about a murder that had been so gruesomely similar to Summer's. So when the trial ends Brandy races from the courthouse to go to her 4:30 p.m. bartending shift at the Marriott. When she gets Connie's call, she turns her car around and heads back to Independence.

* * * * *

Late Friday afternoon Prosecutor Jean Peters Baker walks confidently to the microphone in the conference room at the Jackson County Courthouse in Independence.

"It's a great day," she tells reporters, family members and others gathered in the room. "Justice may be delayed but it's not to be denied." The Prosecutor then briefly outlines the facts surrounding the arrest warrant that has just been delivered to Jeffrey Sauerbry as he was being escorted back to his jail cell following the Kellett murder trial.

"Jeffrey Sauerbry has been charged with first degree murder in the 2004 killing of Summer Shipp," the prosecutor says earnestly. "This proves that it is never too late. He confessed to a friend. He described how he thought she was a spy. He told a friend that he strangled her, cut her throat and dismembered her."

That night a reporter for KMBC TV told his viewers that he had questioned Jean Peters Baker at the press conference, asking her what would have happened if Sauerbry had never opened his mouth, never confessed. Would there have been enough evidence to charge him?

The answer from Baker was a definitive "No."

Despite being exhausted from sitting through the trial, family and friends are exhilarated and relieved that the man they were sure killed their precious Summer would remain behind bars for the rest of his life for the William Kellett murder. But they still wanted justice for Summer Shipp. On that hot August day those supporters who have spent so many years in an agony of unknowing are better off not seeing into the future. They did not know that their day in court would be delayed for another four years. Nor did they suspect that it would not result in the outcome they hoped for.

* * * * *

March, 2016

Ed Rogge pulls the Kia Soul into a parking spot in front of a low building near the Jackson County courthouse. He is worried about how his wife is going to handle this appointment with prosecutors in preparation for the trial of her mother's alleged murderer. Ed has watched Brandy as she shows obvious signs she is feeling more stressed than usual. The tears are just waiting; he knows it won't take much.

Since Ed met Brandy in the winter of 2009 when he showed up at her house to do some weatherizing, he has witnessed endless hours of her physical and psychic pain. She had injured her back moving a portable bar while in her twenties. The lower back pain she lived with since then began intensifying until she had a neurotransmitter installed in 2011, following three back surgeries. For some reason, the electrical pulses that were intended to deaden the pain were not working and the device had to be reprogrammed multiple times. So Brandy spent endless hours lying on the couch, unable to work for more than a half hour, even to type on her computer. She chopped vegetables sitting down and lived her life perched on an ice pack.

The Rogges had married on a beach in Florida on 11-11-11. Aunt Fran had arranged the simple but beautiful ceremony. They returned to Kansas

City and settled into a life of raising purebred Pugs, constantly scouting for construction jobs for Ed and trying to stay on top of Brandy's pain.

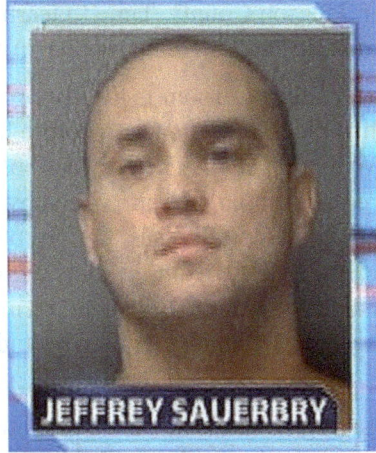

JEFFREY SAUERBRY

It was never easy. Ed had tried to totally brief himself on Brandy's emotional trauma and the details of her mother's murder before and after their wedding. He knew she no longer liked to talk about it or even think about it. As she walks hesitantly into the prosecutor's office and shuts the door behind her, Ed sits on an uncomfortable metal chair and fidgets. He takes one look at her red face and shaking hands 20 minutes later and wonders how in the world she will be able to calm herself enough to testify in the trial that is only a few weeks away.

* * * * *

Brandy Shipp Rogge pops a Xanax into her mouth right before she walks into the courthouse in Independence. She is trying valiantly to keep it together for the trial that will soon start. Jury selection the day before, a Monday, had taken a full day but she and her family and friends had skipped that. They had been told by prosecutors it wasn't necessary for them to be there. Besides, the jury pool was so large there wouldn't have been any room left for spectators. Worse, the stress would have begun a day earlier.

Despite all her mental preparations before the trial, Brandy shakes uncontrollably as she sits with her worried victim's advocate in the hall outside the courtroom.

"I just want to get through my testimony," she says nervously, casting anxious looks in the direction of her dad and Naomi, who are seated on one side of her on the wooden bench outside the courtroom.

"I don't think I can sit through the entire thing," she adds with a deep sigh.

Ed Rogge leans against the wall without saying a word, but he looks just as concerned as the victim's advocate next to Brandy. It is show time in Jackson County. Time to learn what a jury will make of the man they are all sure had killed the mother-in-law he never met.

The courtroom is far from packed. And the defendant looks nothing like the mug shots taken before he was found guilty of the murder of William Kellett. The crewcut bully demeanor of those days has been replaced, no doubt purposely, by a bearded, almost professorial look, complete with glasses, Oxford button-down shirt and a tie that matches one of the defense team's. At his high-powered attorney's insistence, Jeffrey Sauerbry will remain silent during the entire trial, at least partially in keeping with his temporarily studious demeanor.

The Honorable Jack Grate is no stranger to the defendant or the case, having been involved in the original William Kellett murder case before prosecutors dismissed the charges in pre-trial proceedings in November of 2011 and later refiled the case with a new judge. Appointed to the bench in 2004 by then Governor Bob Holden, Judge Grate has practiced law for 28 years in Independence, mostly in a solo practice. Educated as an undergrad at Notre Dame, the judge got his law degree from the University of Missouri-Columbia and worked for a time for Legal Aid of Western Missouri after being a partner in an Independence law firm. While his spectacled wide face and thinning gray hair hint at benevolence, Judge Jack Grate shows he is all serious business as he opens the trial with the customary admonitions and instructions to the jury.

"The defense attorney does not need to make a statement if he does not choose. This case must be decided only on the evidence presented here–not from other places. Do not let blogs, tweets or any other source be consulted. Do not take your notes out of the courtroom. Do not share them with anyone. Do not rely on your notes. Once you reach a verdict, your notes are destroyed. Disregard the things the court asks you to disregard."

With the preliminaries out of the way, the black-robed judge sits back to preside over one of the most high profile cases ever to be heard in the Independence courthouse.

Prosecutor Traci Stansell begins her case by introducing the jury to Summer Shipp, displaying photos of her on a screen and outlining the early days of her disappearance. She leads the jury to the day of Summer's disappearance, noting that Jeffrey Sauerbry had made his way to the front porch of his neighbor's house right after Summer had left. Bill Summers had told the woman doing marketing surveys that he wasn't interested.

As Jeffrey Sauerbry tried to sell him on a phone service a few minutes later, Summers remarked to Sauerbry, "It looks like you are about to have company."

"Summer Shipp was never seen alive again," says Prosecutor Stansell. Another Independence neighbor later told police looking for the woman to talk to Jeffrey Sauerbry. Despite dog searches, search warrants executed on Jeffrey's house and vehicles, helicopter searches and foot searches, there was no sign of Summer until October of 2007, when two fishermen found her skull. After another exhaustive search in the waters of the Little Blue River, only a few traces of Summer Shipp turned up–bones and clothing. But what was found was enough to identify her; just some long bones and a vertebrae. From those bones the medical examiner determined that her death occurred by homicide.

"Now we know where Summer is, but we don't know how she got there...until 2012," Stansell continues outlining the state's case. "During the course of another investigation we found out a man named Darrell Wilson knew what happened. Because Jeffrey Sauerbry told him. This witness did not want to come forward but he did. And the tale he told was chilling."

The prosecutor says that Jeffrey Sauerbry told Darrell Wilson that Summer Shipp had come to his house, that he had choked her, slit her throat and dismembered her. Stansell concludes her opening statement by outlining the testimony the jury will hear during the trial; testimony to be given by people who have worked tirelessly to get the case to this point so Summer could have justice.

Defense Attorney Joe Piceno uses an old fashioned flip chart for his opening statement, rather than a Power Point presentation.

"Ninety-nine percent of what the prosecutor just told you we have no disagreement with," he begins. He tells the jury that, despite three separate searches of his client's house and truck, there was no evidence Summer Shipp had been in either place. He cautions the jury to pay attention to important dates, especially in regard to the prosecution's key witness, Darrell Wilson, since they don't match things as they actually occurred. He reports that Darrell's sister, Diana Reno Huffman, had been the key witness in another Sauerbry trial. Picerno also points out that Wilson reportedly said, when he talked to police about the current case, that he had told his sister about Sauerbry's confession. "Yet Diana Huffman told police nothing about Jeffrey Sauerbry's confession. Not one word."

"There is no burden to prove motive on the defense," Picerno cautions. "Darrell Wilson has four prior felony convictions. He was a snitch, out to get deals for himself. So I will ask you to evaluate his credibility. Keep in mind what kind of person he is and what his goal was–reward money. You can't believe him because what he told the state does not comport with the facts of the case. There is no way that what he claimed took place. I will ask for a not guilty verdict."

Brandy is the first witness for the state and outlines the timeline of her mother's disappearance and the subsequent search for her. She talks about the website the family set up and the reward funds that were pledged but never given out to anyone. She completes her testimony calmly, without tears, and leaves the courtroom. Her family does not expect her to return, but getting through the ordeal has apparently been a relief, since she shows up in the courtroom spectator section right after the first break.

Still, Brandy soon finds it almost unbearable as crime scene investigators detail the evidence found in the river in 2007, beginning with an initial water search on December 7 by the Lee's Summit Search and Rescue team in full body dry suits. In later searches the rescue team found a piece of cloth and a plastic bag. They found a Jeans pocket, a bra and a scarf during that first day. In later searches the rescue team found seven more bones, including a pelvis, ribs and vertebrae, to add to the skull, mandible, jawbone and long bone found the first day. Prosecutor Stansell places the clothing items on the ledge in front of the jury as she elicits the information from the investigator that subsequent excavations in the river area found no more traces of Summer Shipp.

In Picerno's cross examination, he emphasizes the searches conducted on Sauerbry's vehicle had uncovered no trace evidence and asks for a copy of a deposition to refresh the memory of the crime scene investigator he questions.

When the case resumes after an 11:00 a.m. recess, Dr. Michael Finnigan, a forensic anthropologist, takes the stand and outlines the reports he had given to Dr. Mary Dudley with the Jackson County Medical Examiner's office. His testimony is followed by questioning of the Independence neighbors who had seen or talked to Summer Shipp the day she went missing.

Dr. Diane Peterson, the county's current chief medical examiner, next gives testimony on the independent analysis she had performed on Summer Shipp's remains. She had looked at photographs, diagrams, autopsy reports and all the reports related to the case. In commenting on photographs shown to the jury, Dr. Peterson shows a closeup photo of what she terms a "blue stick fracture," which is a fracture not going through the entire bone but similar to the way one can slice a green twig but not get through the entire twig. Dr. Peterson surmises it was likely that the fracture happened in life, and as there were no signs of healing; the break occurred just prior to death.

Dr. Peterson has also determined the cause of death is homicidal violence, due to the body being recovered in a river instead of at the same place the individual disappeared. She notes the rib fracture, as well as the scarf found near the bones which was tied into a very small loop. That loop was not a typical way to wear a scarf and led the medical examiner to believe it was possible the scarf had been used to strangle the victim.

"For it to be found with her remains tells me it did belong to her," says Dr. Peterson. "It tells me there is a connection over and above simply being recovered with the bones." She adds that the bra and jeans pocket found near the bones were of a small size, fitting the size of the victim.

Dr. Peterson's testimony is suddenly interrupted by the attorneys approaching the judge's bench. The jury is asked to leave the courtroom while Picerno argues that if the medical examiner can not associate the scarf definitively with Summer Shipp, then the cause and manner of death will have to be indeterminate instead of homicide. When the jury returns, a subdued and seemingly frustrated Dr. Peterson reluctantly changes her ruling on the cause of death to "indeterminate."

* * * * *

The second day of the trial brings the testimony of the state's key witness, Darrell Wilson. Right away the prosecutor asks him about his prior criminal convictions, including charges of intent to manufacture a controlled substance, possession with the intent to distribute a controlled substance and use of a communications facility to commit a controlled substance offense. Wilson admits to the violations and also admits to DWI convictions. When asked how he knows the defendant, Wilson says he's known Sauerbry through a nephew since he was ten or 12 years old. He then recalls, at the prosecution's questioning, the night Jeffrey Sauerbry came to his house at 1814 Redwood Drive in Independence to get on the computer to look at dating sites. Instead of the chat rooms he had promised to look at, Wilson found Sauerbry had a "whole screen full about Summer Shipp." When Wilson asked Sauerbry about it he told him that Summer Shipp had come to his house and he had thought she was a CIA operative. So he snatched her, got her inside, strangled her and cut her throat. Wilson then said Sauerbry told him he had chopped her up and put her in trash bags.

Wilson further states that the next time he saw Sauerbry was at Wilson's mother's funeral, since Sauerbry was one of the pallbearers. Wilson added that he had told his mother and sister about Sauerbry's confession but did not repeat the confession story until 2012, when two detectives came knocking on his door. He had not come forward with his story before then because, he said, he was scared.

When Picerno's turn comes to cross-examine Wilson, he asks the witness about his work as a confidential informant for the Drug Enforcement Agency. When Wilson replies that he was not an informant, Picerno refers him to a deposition in which Wilson had admitted he wore a wire and talked to people about committing crimes to gain their confidence. When pressed by Picerno about a burglary conviction, Wilson becomes obviously agitated, claims he only has one federal conviction and that one of his drug cases was reversed. When the defense attorney presses Wilson about when the confession by Jeffrey Sauerbry had occurred, noting discrepancies in dates, Wilson admits he got confused.

Then the angry witness says, "By God, he killed that woman! He chopped her up and threw her away like garbage!"

When the State rests following Wilson's testimony, Picerno asks for a stipulation that funeral services for Wilson's mother occurred in 2009, rather than in 2008 as Wilson has claimed. The defense calls no witnesses and the judge issues jury instructions before closing arguments.

Assistant Prosecutor Jeremy Baldwin defends Darrell Wilson in the state's first closing statement. "Darrell Wilson is a most matter-of-fact guy. He got pissed off, he yelled. He talked about his mama dying. He got mad. Think about what he said and how he said it. He took a beating and stood strong, because that's what happened. Yes, he's got priors. The state doesn't pick who Jeffrey Sauerbry confessed to. Can you believe him? You know as you sit there, you can believe him."

Baldwin continues, "The state presents to you that Jeff is the murder weapon. When you go to deliberate, ask for all the physical evidence. Remember, it's a 13-minute drive from Sauerbrry's house to the Little Blue River where Summer Shipp's body was dumped . . . three left turns. She was a CIA operative, so he killed her. "

When Picerno's turn comes, he reminds the jurors about what he claimed was only circumstantial evidence. "You just heard a lot of summation with no facts to them. There is no way around it. In order to convict, you must believe Darrell Wilson. There is no other way."

The defense notes that Jeffrey Sauerbry was a person of interest in the Summer Shipp case since day one, but there was never enough probable cause to arrest him for the crime. "Jeff happened to be there when Summer was going door-to-door. Premeditation is preposterous."

Picerno continues, "The state opened the case with the manner of death homicidal violence, but the medical expert could not say she died of homicidal violence. Instead, it is undetermined. We don't know it was a homicide. We can only speculate."

He continues to hammer away at Wilson's testimony. "Not one single person should take his word. He can't be trusted for a lot of different reasons. He doesn't know what the hell happened."

Picerno concludes, "There is no evidence of anything. You must find him not guilty."

When Traci Stansell presents the State's closing statement, she notes, "Ninety percent of Summer disappeared and is gone forever because of what this man did. He made sure that is all we would have, and thank God we had enough to identify her. . . . If that ten percent of her hadn't been caught, her daughter would never have been able to put her to rest."

Stansell admits that Darrell Wilson is by no means a perfect human being, yet he voluntarily put himself through "what he just went through at the hands of Mr. Picerno."

She concludes, "The man who confessed to Darrell Wilson just happened to live on the street, in the same house that she was last seen. Don't reward Jeffrey Sauerbry for covering his tracks and for making sure that very little of Summer Shipp would be found, for being a good criminal. He is a murderer. Summer was an innocent victim. She was doing her job and only 140 feet away from going home and seeing her daughter again. Until she went to the wrong house."

* * * *

In almost an exact repeat of the William Kellett murder trial, witnesses and police officers cram themselves into the Independence courtroom on Wednesday, standing along the wall in the back because the seats are all occupied. The jury has deliberated for just under two hours when they file in and the foreman hands the verdict envelope to the bailiff. The verdict, however, is not a repeat of the Kellet case.

When Judge Grate reads the not-guilty verdict, Jeffrey Sauerbry collapses onto the table where he sits between the defense team members, sobbing uncontrollably.

Brandy Shipp and her family and friends join the police officers and investigators as they file out of the courtroom in a stunned, quiet disbelief.

Chapter 17 - Life Without Summer

April 26, 2016

Late in the afternoon of April 26 Brandy Shipp stands outside the courthouse annex in Independence, minutes after the acquittal of Jeffrey Sauerbry. She faces the TV camera without tears, her long red hair blowing in a stiff breeze. She admits to the off-camera reporter that she had known, going into the trial, the state would have a tough time proving beyond a reasonable doubt that Sauerbry had murdered her mother. There just wasn't enough tangible evidence connecting him to the long-ago deed, even though the confession to his friend and all the other circumstantial evidence was strong.

"In our hearts we all know Sauerbry killed her," she says, looking bravely into the camera. "It doesn't really matter what those 12 people think. For us, it's a good thing he won't be able to do anything like this to anybody else. At least he's off the streets."

Back in the courtroom, Jeffrey Sauerbry is being escorted to a prison van after changing back into jail scrubs and surrendering the borrowed street clothes that had helped him look like a normal, harmless guy.

A few hours later Glen Crawford, an alternate juror in the case, tells reporters that he and the other alternate felt the jury had "got it wrong." Outside the courthouse he had waited to speak to Brandy Shipp until after she was finished with a television crew. He told her that none of the jurors knew Jeffrey Sauerbry had already been convicted of another murder. They knew nothing about any of his past criminal activities. If they had known, he was sure that would have changed the verdict.

Later that day Brandy shakes off the stress of the past few weeks, months and years, telling newspaper reporters who call for her comments that the trial did not give her closure. There would never, ever be closure. Still, she intends to somehow keep her mother's story alive.

She had left the courthouse with a good friend from Colorado who had come into town to support her during the trial. They were both going to Brandy's house to decompress.

* * * * *

Before the Summer Shipp case Malisa Jennings had been a relatively happy, fairly anonymous resident of Independence, Missouri. Ironically, she had taken a few surveys that were conducted by the marketing firm that Summer worked for, but never with Summer. She would have remembered someone that effervescent and beautiful, that sensitive and loving.

And Malisa can now sympathize so much with what Brandy Shipp has gone through, because she lost her husband to a tragic death in 2015. Malisa now lives with anxiety and depression on a daily basis. Her brush with the Shipp murder case makes the pain of loss even more acute somehow. It has intensified all her fears—fears that she had never felt before Jeffery Sauerbry and those evil, dark eyes appeared in front of her that day in Nick's.

Today it seems like it's getting harder to remember who she was before she began looking over her shoulder after that first encounter with Sauerbry and the many that followed. Even though she knows the man will never be free to walk the streets again, she fears that he knows too many people and that she won't know at any given time if she's talking to one of his acquaintances. Maybe someone who could start stalking her the way Sauerbry stalked her.

Every morning when she wakes up, Malisa is still the person she was forced to become through all of this. But now there are no reassuring arms to hold her, no voice in her ear telling her that everything will be okay, no love to drown out the fear. Her husband is gone. This is her new reality.

* * * * *

Like so many of the women that Summer Shipp impacted during her prematurely-ended life, Mary Lynn Bass also continues to be haunted emotionally by the loss of her friend and the poignant moments they shared. M.L., as she calls herself professionally, became acquainted with Summer through husband John and the film industry he and M.L. both work in. She was not part of Summer's hat party group, but had been invited to many of her back yard parties.

M.L. had been working 12- to 14-hour days on a TV series in Dallas when she got a call from Brandy back in December 2004. She asked M.L. if she and her mother were on some adventure together. In retrospect, both Brandy and M.L. knew she was clutching at straws in the opening days of the search for Summer.

Summer's disappearance has been especially difficult for M.L to swallow, somehow causing her to have flashbacks to the mugging she endured in Kansas City before she moved to L.A. And while she had grown up in the family funeral business in Illinois and was certainly acquainted with death, Summer's murder hit her extra hard. It became even more difficult to endure in 2014 when she moved back to Kansas City and was shown a document that described how Summer's accused murderer had allegedly taken her down. M.L. knows the stages of grief, but this death of a friend is so much worse than she could have imagined. She is especially worried now about how the prolonged searching and agony Brandy had suffered through the trial will affect her in the long term.

But the writer in this film writer-producer kicks into gear as M.L. decides to focus on the positives of Summer's life. She has to write about it. She has to preserve the memories, at least for herself, after sitting through one of the days of the trial in support of Brandy. She turns to Facebook, knowing that Summer's friends and their mutual film acquaintances will see it and perhaps also come to terms with her impact on all their lives.

"Yesterday, a gal in aqua aerobics class said I looked dead. Admittedly, I have not been my normal animated self, but dead? I paused, then realized a piece of me died again during the trial regarding Summer Shipp's murder," M.L. wrote in her Facebook post.

"I know she would want me to enjoy being in the water again and living life to its fullest. And I know she would not want me thinking, or others thinking, only about the way she died; but rather about how she lived so fully in wonderment and joy of life's simple pleasures. She would not want people to stop talking with strangers, disengage from one another or live in fear. She celebrated the serendipitous encounters with all kinds of people because it comprised a large part of the richness of her life experience. I know she would want us all to be richer in that off-line, old fashioned, old school way of being friendly out in the world with one another. And I know she would want us all smiling at one another, with her trademark glint of impish delight, for no apparent reason other than the recognition of connection of spirits sharing fleeting moments of joy.

So, I'm going to post a letter here that I wrote from LA in 2007 and then I'm going to return to remembering and reflecting the rays of warm sunshine Summer cast around all of us who loved her so dearly and miss her so very much.

Searching for Summer

Dear family and friends,

I woke up in LA today with several messages about Summer in my inbox. It's a very sad day. And it's been especially hard being away from you all during the years since her disappearance. It feels terribly lonely to deal with this; unable to gather and hug one another.

The last time Summer and I were together, I was in KC on business and recovering from being mugged. We were enjoying swimming and talking in my friend's swimming pool. She was wearing one of those 60's swimming caps with the plastic flower petals that jiggle with every movement. I hadn't seen one of those in decades and it took me back to my childhood with summers spent at the pool, without a care in the world.

I scolded her for not returning my voice-mail messages and making me worry about her. Then she told me that her mother had died and she had been back in Illinois (close to where I was born). We talked about our mothers and how you're never really prepared for the experience of losing them.

Summer could swim long after I ran out of steam. So, like the former water safety instructor in me, I stood and studied her freestyle technique. And I watched that dance between the floral design in her suit and her hat, and marveled at her ability to balance form and fashion function–even under water!

I had previously shown her a show stopping floral summer dress and jacket ensemble that I had recently splurged on and paid 35 bucks for at the wonderful, if not over-priced, Junior League thrift store. She loved it so much that we decided to share it. Then we got a crazy idea to go to a big fundraising function together. Would we "premier" it at Warren Buffett's event or at the opening of the Veteran's Memorial? Whatever the function, one of us would wear it for the first half, then switch clothes halfway so that the other one could have fun watching reactions and create some talk.

Then we took our brainstorming one step further and decided to sell "shares" of the outfit to other women for $5 each and have them showing up all over town for all sorts of summertime functions. (It had a stretchable bodice and a puffy hip design–so virtually anyone from size 2 to 20 could wear it). Summer already had fabulous accessories in mind for it, which she brought that day. We were giddy over the outfit and the idea; its accessorizing possibilities, the dazzlingly original economic and social model of ownership (even Warren might be able to appreciate that!) and *the significant social and artistic statements all of our smart girlfriends could make, regardless of size! Democracy in dressing– we're starting a movement now!*

Somewhere in the middle of it all she declared that I was "the most creative person she had ever known." I was dumbfounded because she knows every creative person in Kansas City. But, it was a typical Summer statement–giving someone else the credit and star light for something she clearly collaborated on at the highest level.

Today, upon receiving the news that she was found in the waters of Little Blue, I wish I had asked Brandy to save that dress.

Now I see that I could have actualized our crazy, yet wonderful idea. And we could have kept Summer's spirit alive in many social circles and at many gatherings for years to come. It could have been known as "THE SUMMER Dress."

She was the kind of girl (and it was the kind of outfit) that makes you smile from the moment she walks into the room 'til she makes her exit.

* * * * *

Just as there was no closure after the trial, Brandy has found there is little to keep her grounded now that she has lost one of her main life purposes. She often turns her focus inward, spending hours sprawled on the couch in a stupor, coping unsuccessfully with back pain and psychic trauma. She and Ed still pour all their love into every litter of Pug puppies they raise in their home in Kansas City. Ed tries to keep the construction jobs coming in to maintain a steady income. But the couple struggles financially.

They thought things couldn't get any worse after the trial, but they were wrong. Brandy hasn't worked since 2012. The pain in her back has escalated to the point where she cannot stand or sit any longer than ten minutes without being in agony.

What are they to do now? One day, despite the pain, Brandy begs Ed to drive her to Iberia to visit her mother's grave. She needs to take flowers to Summer. She needs to talk to her mother, to somehow sense her presence near the only physical evidence of her that remains. Ed resists initially, knowing the drama that will ensue, but he finally agrees to the trip.

Yes, there is drama, once they arrive at the cemetery. And of course there are tears . . . hiccupping, guttural sobbing that shakes her to the core, more than the sum of all previous crying episodes. Brandy collapses onto the tombstone, clawing at the ground in bitterness. She cries for all her losses, all her mistakes and missteps. She apologizes to her mother, first for not being able to protect her from her innocent trust of everyone, then for not being able to find her. And finally, for not being able to help vindicate her murder with a conviction.

As she places red roses on the ground in front of the beautiful tombstone, a dry exhaustion sets in. But then Brandy recalls the words her mother had supposedly spoken through a psychic that a friend had called from the courthouse as the family waited for the jury verdict at the murder trial.

"Live your life," Summer had told the psychic to tell Brandy. But her words right before that had been aimed at instructing the way the story of Summer's life should be written. "Just the facts, ma'am," Summer had said in her dry wit, imitating the voice of Sergeant Joe Friday, her favorite fictional character on the old TV show, **Dragnet.**

Ok. So there was that, Brandy muses on the way home. There is Summer's story. She needs to preserve her mother's memory somehow.

Brandy decides she will finally begin accepting invitations to the regular lunches her mother's friends always have in Summer's honor. She will join them in raising a toast to her precious mother, to friendship, to hope. Summer would love that.

Brandy then realizes that by visiting the elderly woman she and Ed are always helping she is doing exactly what her mother would be doing if she were still alive. She had always brought forgotten or ill folks under her protection and care.

And of course there are the dogs to focus on. She and Ed love their Pugs as much as Summer loved all her rescued and stray animals.

As they get closer to Kansas City, Brandy also vows to plant roses in their yard. She smiles wryly as she hears the echo of her mother's voice in her future as she now becomes the one to ask . . . maybe even demand . . . her family and friends stop to smell the roses.

Epilogue

January in Granite City, Illinois can freeze your soul. It's as gray and cold as the steel in the mill yards there.

When Summer arrived in January, over a half century ago, her warmth brightened the lives and souls of those who would come to know her. The birth of this golden source of light and energy inspired a sense of summer, even in the dead of winter. The joy of the child, the travails of the woman, brought a steady flow of inspiration to all, then and throughout all of our lives. I, like each of the others in our close group of friends, became and remain one of "Summer's Girls."

We all became infused with the warm, spirited love Summer brought to each of us. We joyously, proudly say we are Summer's Girls, not as a possession, but more as a work in progress, revitalized by her undying gifts. We are so much better for it. Always!

This memoir of Summer Shipp came to me as a draft for my review. Good friends have bolstered me through my professional path of writing and editing/producing for years. The manuscript, from a good friend, drew me from my daily production load just as Summer's smile would always call me to attention. Her memory, her ever-present spirit, remains a daily conversation I enter into comfortably for strength, encouragement and to fight those fears of completion. One of her many gifts to me is the good example of never caving into fear.

Through a day and night of distraction, sensations of Summer's presence, and memories of my own fights against grief and tragedy, I finished reading the manuscript. I then wrote to Summer's daughter and ex-husband:

Dear Brandy and John;

I would not be able to put Summer's story down even as a complete stranger. It artfully weaves the story of one woman's gift of capturing light so as to bring your focus upon the best in humanity amidst the sea of disturbance and tragedy, achieving an enduring fabric of human kindness and potential. No name, no label comes to mind for that genetically good, old fashioned, spiritual essence that is Summer. We remain inspired by her to fulfill every moment in life. In my own life, as a child of funeral directors, the words of so many who had lived safe, measured, untraveled and unadventurous lives have stayed with me. Those words helped me see what Summer knew all along: connecting in person-with loved ones and strangers- was the sweet spot in life, a life well lived. A devoted mother and friend, she left us with a ready made community to hold each other tight when we think her light has been extinguished. It has not!

Sending this note filled me with renewed hope that Summer Shipp's sunshine will forever warm Summer's Girls and continue to bring peace to my sometimes weary soul.

May each and every reader of Summer Shipp's life wonder then: If I disappear tomorrow, what kind of posse will come looking for me? What kind of love, passion, imagination or delight in living have I stirred in people so that they would drop everything to go to the ends of the earth to find me?

As for this member of Summer's Girls, it's "Posse Inspiring Time"!

Mary Lynn (M.L.) Bass

Summer's Girls . . . some of the women who still gather in honor and memory of Summer Shipp

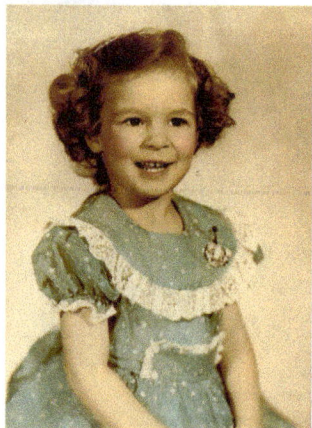

*Images from
Summer Shipp's
childhood and
early adulthood.*

*Summer and
her mother and
extended family
members*

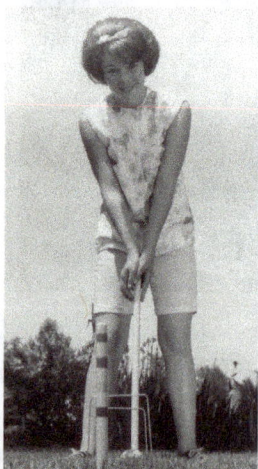

Summer at the Bijou Theater, with Brandy, and at a local art fair

SUMMER SHIPP | Family and friends come together for a celebration of her life

Daughter turns grief into hope for others

An overflow crowd fills a theater to share memories of the woman whose remains were recently found.

By DONALD BRADLEY and GENE MEYER
The Kansas City Star

For three years after Summer Shipp disappeared from an Independence neighborhood where she had been doing a door-to-door survey, her daughter clung to the hope that her mother was still alive.

There never was any good news to feed Brandy Shipp's hope. No credible sightings or leads about her mother. As time passed, there was never a reason, really, to think the outcome would be different than what it turned out to be: Her mother was dead, probably murdered.

"But she was my mother, and I kept hoping that ... maybe she was out there somewhere ... brainwashed or something," Brandy said at the dining table in her father's home in Waldo. "That's what I was down to."

Hope — desperate hope — comes from the heart, not the brain, she said.

"I don't think we ever get the choice to give that up."

SEE SHIPP | B4

DAVID EULITT | THE KANSAS CITY STAR

A capacity crowd at the Screenland Theatre in Kansas City on Saturday attended a memorial service for Summer Shipp. Brandy Shipp (center), Summer Shipp's daughter, closed her eyes during a song by musician David Basse. With Brandy Shipp were her father, John Shipp, and his wife, Naomi Shipp.

Photo reproduced by permission of The Kansas City Star

The True Spirit of Community

The authors and the family of Summer Shipp sincerely thank all those individuals and organizations assisting with the search and investigation and with so many other acts of support and comfort. In the names that appear below, those individuals and businesses playing a significant role in this story are in bold, followed by page numbers where they are mentioned.

From the depths of our hearts, we want to thank you wonderful people and organizations for the incredible love and support you've shown us. And to the hundreds of others not listed, we thank you, too. The search for Summer brought out the true spirit of community and love.

Aide Andrew

Alberta Kleitz–88

Al Shoaf

Al Sokol

Alice Diederich

Alycia Daniels

Alise Martiny

Alison Conrad

Alonzo Washington–99

Alvin Brooks–6, 48, 102,104

Amanda Rodriquez

Amy Bills

Amy Schwartz

Anita Campbell–77

Anita Leone

Anita Shore

Anita Strub

Ann Garcia

Special thanks to Naomi

While sitting on the deck with Anne and my Dad to finalize this story, Naomi opened the last book proof and quickly corrected a small typographical error. Suddenly it dawned on me that Naomi Shipp has done more than anyone realizes. She, the silent, wonderful person in the background doing so much, never wanted any acknowledgement or appreciation, yet she was always there. She never asked "What can I do?" She just did. No words can describe how much I appreciate everything she did so unselfishly and full-heartedly for my Dad and me through these confusing, turbulent, and unpredictable years. She is a one-of-a-kind hero and I love her more than she'll ever know.

–Brandy Shipp Rogge

Claude Page

Claudia Short

Connie Gauger–35

Connie Perucca

Connie Vitale–52, 74

Corilyn Hensel

Dale Keene–78

Daniel Bartle–83, 84

Dan Hernandez

Dan Hurst

Dan Verbeck

Dan Viets

Daniel Eshnaur

Dana Poindexter

Danny McCullough

Darcie Blake

Darlene Burril

Daryl Smith

Dave Munday

David Basse–102

David McCabe

David Naster

David Schmidt

David Shipp

David Yonally–74

David Van Norman

Debbie Bevan

Debbie Kelley

Deborah Scott

Debra West–57

Dede Keene–78

Dee Sexton–87

Deidra Chase

Delbert Kelley

Delores Loutzenhiser

Delores Smith

Demi Gerow

Dennis Green

Dennis Stofferahn

Desiree Hugill-Houston

Det. Jana Rogge

Det. Terry Dorman

Devin Kelley

Diane Mares

Dianne Gutin

Dick Wilson

Dina Michaels

DJ Nolen

Dodie Murphy–79

Dina Michaels

Don Lyon

Don Maxwell–82, 88

Donald Roberts

Donald Wright

Donna Pitman

Doris Scott

Dot Tarantino

Doug and Mary Lyall

Searching for Summer

Michael Cullinan

Michael Derby

Michael Gettino

Michael Madrigal

Michele Staponski-Howell

Michelle Cox

Mike Heft

Mike Johann

Mike Murphy

Mike Schwartz

Milica Milakovich

Monica Caison

Nancy Cipolla–60

Neil Bernard–86

Nick DiGirlamo

Norma Jean Chennell

Olga Marr

Ouida Touchon

Pat Gallagher

Patricia Kieffer

Patrick Michaels

Paulla Levitch

Pen Smith

Penny Valladares

Phillip Cacioppo

Phyllis Hamrick

Randy Nagel–68

Rey Barbosa

Ric Tucker

Richard Ambler

Richard Lotman Brown

Richard Vick

Rita Lechtenberg

Rob & Erin Hall

Robert Hite

Robert Hudson

Robert Serra

Rochelle Stoloff

Rocky Leavitt

Roger Kemp

Roger Walters

Ron Rooks

Ronald Cox

Ronda Montgomery

Ronnie Rocket

Rossana Jeran

Rose and Leo Eilts

Russ Ptacek

Russ Pulley

Ruth Simison

Sam Mann

Scarlett Barbosa

Scarlett Gerow

Scotti Bickford–81, 19

Scott Burnett

Scott Carroll

Scott Twyman

Shannon Kelley

Sharlette John

Sharon Owen

Searching for Summer

Sharon Rapoport

Shawna Williams

Sherry Schmidt

Skid Roadie

Stephanie & Chris Oehlert

Stephanie Boothe

Stephen Durbin

Stephen Schneider

Steve McGown

Steve Simpson

Steven Whitacre

Stuart Gethner

Susan Dill

Sue Herrick–54, 75

Susan Dill

Susan Lawrence–28, 83, 79

Susan Sarachek

Susan Smith

Suzanne Gordon

Suzi Perkins

Sylvia Stone

T. Max Graham

Tammy Dickinson

Tammy Navinskey

Tanna Guthrie

Tennyson Salmon

Teresa Reiss

Terry Sprick

Tess Koppelman

Terry Dorman

The Marble Lady

Theresa Leavitt

Tina Porter

Tom Finley–82

Tom McLean

Tracy Guenther

Tracy Holmes

Travis Forbes

Travis Taylor

Vanessa Allen

Vinh Phan

Walter Klammer

Wanda Cogburn

Wendy Doyle

Wendy Gray

Wes Jeffries

Wes Neal

Yung Joo Kim

Businesses and Organizations

Achieve Foundation

American Medical Response

America's Missing, Abducted & Lost Persons, Beaumont, TX–78

America's Most Wanted

Assistance in Research

Back Pages

Bloomsday Books

Blue River Police

Boulevard Drive-In Theater

C.C.I. Agency

CBS (Viacom) Billboard Co.

Center For Hope, Albany, NY

Cinema Consultants, Inc.

Classic Cup Employees

Clayman & Gunter Attorneys

CUE Center for Missing Persons, Wilmington, NC–150

Custom Color Corporation

Dickinson Theatres

Essential Market Research

Eye on Independence Newsletter

Fasone Garrett Marketing

Film Society of Greater KC

First Federal Bank, NKC

Hairstyle, Inc.

HOT 103 JAMZ

Independence Examiner

Independence Police Department–5,33, 37, 53, 62, 93, 107

Independence Police Volunteers

Independence Public Works

Interviewing Greater K.C., Inc.

Jackson County Sheriff's Department

K.C. Area Drive-In Theatres

Kansas City Crime Lab

Kansas City Star

Kansas City Urban Core Group

KC Area Transportation Authority

KCMO 710 Talk Radio

KCTV 5 News

Ken Bu Kan-Real Karate

KKFI 90.1

KMBC Channel 9 News

KMBZ 980 AM

KSHB Channel 41 News

KUDL 98.1

KY 99.7

Lamar Advertising

Lee's Summit Underwater Rescue & Recovery–124

Magic 107.3

Majestic Theatres

Mesa Wraps

Metropolitan Community College Police Fire Cadets

Mix 93.3

Montel Williams Show

MOVE-UP Foundation

Nancy Grace Show

CNN Headline News

National Center for Missing Adults

Parkville Antique Mall

Penn Valley Community College

Spectrum

Pitch Weekly

Project Jason, Omaha, NE–62

Quicken Loans

Rebar, Inc.

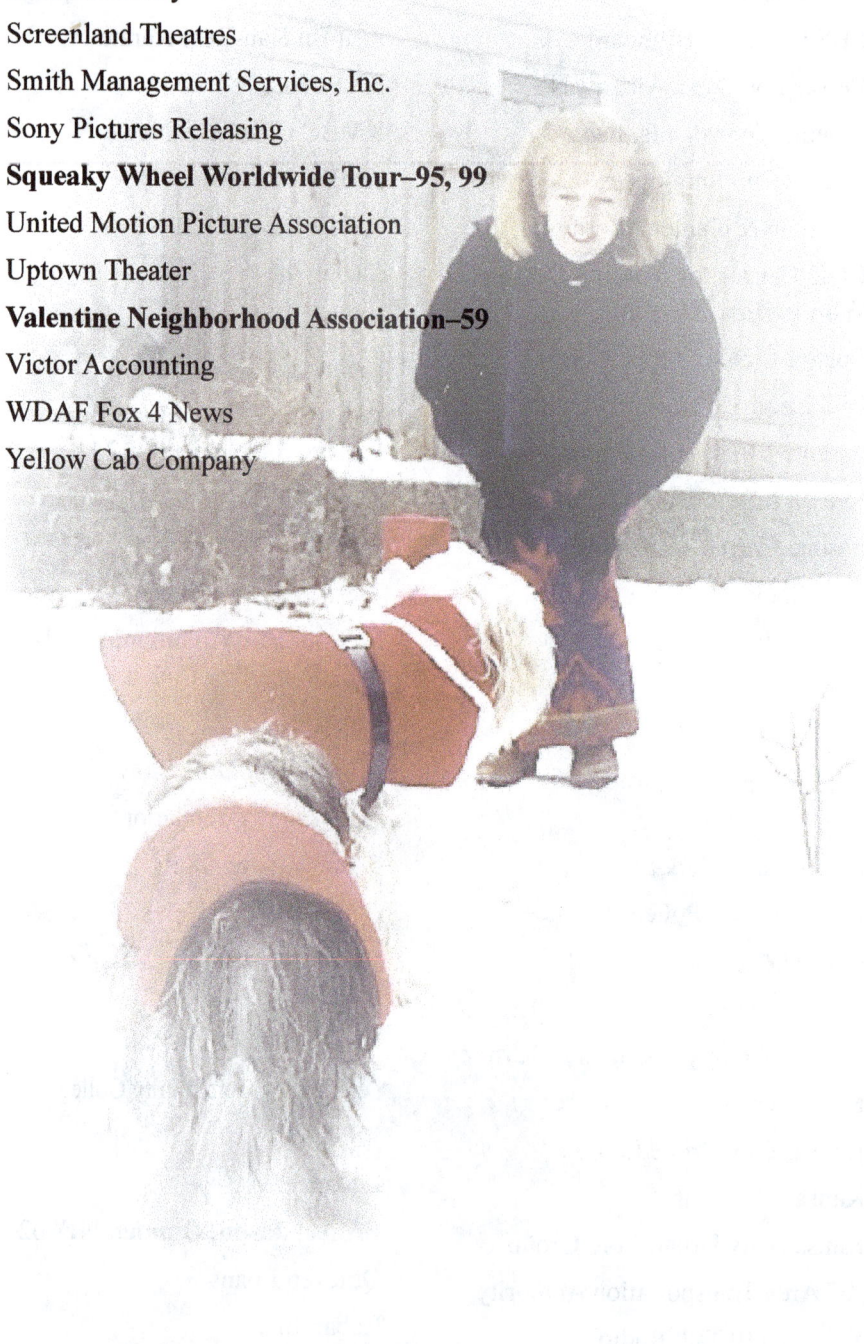

About the CUE Center for Missing Persons

A total of 5% of the profit from each copy of this book sold will be donated to the Cue Center for Missing Persons. This is the organization that Brandy Shipp turned to for expertise and emotional support during the search for Summer.

Community United Effort, also known as CUE, is a 501c3 tax exempt non-profit organization founded in Wilmington, North Carolina. The organization has provided advocacy for missing children and adults since 1994. The organization also provides free, professionally-trained searching, personal and victim support service. The Center has helped more than 12,000 families in what is often the most confusing and desperate times of their lives.

The all-volunteer CUE Center includes students, law enforcement, business leaders and professionally trained field search teams and missing person experts. There are no paid employees, including the founder, Monica Caison, who receives no salary.

A statement on the CUE website notes:

We recognize this silent crisis as we press forward to bring these issues to the forefront across the country and continue to reveal the pain and agony families are forced to face, fully understanding that it's the unknown fate of an individual that leaves communities devastated. In 2016, there were 650,000 missing person reports nationwide. We strive to make the difference daily for those who struggle to endure the challenges concerning a missing loved one. Because of our supporters we are able to help lighten the load for families left behind.

Monica Caison adds that empowerment is what the families receive from CUE events and volunteers. They also receive education and understanding on such topics as who is working on the cases, even behind the scenes. At CUE events, the family members can share their experiences and give law enforcement professionals an understanding of why they need to know the status of their cases so quickly.

One man told Caison, "This is the only place I can laugh out loud." She explains that everyone in the CUE family understands that while he is still grieving, he needs moments of levity and normalcy during that process.

CUE has had many successful conclusions to cases, including the case of a mentally ill man who had disappeared and was found by CUE volunteers through a local newspaper. "He came to our conference that year with his family to thank us," says Caison.

CUE has the resources to start a major campaign when a loved one disappears. And the organization has come a long way with new technology to aid in the searches. However, Caison explains that training and education of law enforcement is a hit and miss process, especially in rural communities that lack funding.

CUE has a college internship program and an online store, with proceeds from all purchases helping fund active searches. The organization can be reached by phoning 910-343-1131 or by emailing cuecenter@aol.com. The mailing address is: Community United Effort, P. O. Box 12714, Wilmington, North Carolina 28405.

www.ingramcontent.com/pod-product-compliance
Lightning Source LLC
Chambersburg PA
CBHW050233270326
41914CB00033BB/1903/J

* 9 7 8 1 7 3 3 0 2 6 6 0 4 *